PENGUIN BOOKS

ROMANTIC NEW ORLEANS

Deirdre Stanforth's first professional career was as a commercial artist and illustrator, but as she is the daughter of Tess Crager, owner of the fabled Basement Bookshop in New Orleans, it was perhaps inevitable that she would eventually turn to writing as well. Born in New Orleans, Mrs. Stanforth earned her Bachelor of Arts degree at Newcomb College there and did graduate work at the Tyler Art School in Philadelphia. Several of her earlier books are on subjects associated with New Orleans, including *Creole!* and the often reprinted *New Orleans Restaurant Cookbook*. She is the illustrator (and coauthor, with Hermann B. Deutsch) of the highly successful *Brennan's New Orleans Cookbook*. With Martha Stamm, she wrote *Buying and Renovating a House in the City*, based on their own experiences with old houses in New York City. The success of this venture inspired Mrs. Stanforth to write *Restored America*, illustrated with photographs by Louis Reens. Mrs. Stanforth is vice-president of the Brownstone Revival Committee in New York City and a member of the Advisory Committee of the Carlyle House Council of Alexandria, Virginia. She and her husband, James D. Stanforth, live in New York City.

Louis Reens is one of America's leading architectural photographers. In addition to his illustrations for *Restored America*, his pictures appeared in *Young Designs in Living* and *Young Designs in Color* by Barbara Plumb, *Home* by Letitia Baldrige, *Living for Today* by Karen Fisher, *The New York Times Book of Interior Design and Decoration* by George O'Brien, and numerous other books. From 1957 to 1975 he was a staff photographer for *Interiors* magazine, and he has contributed photographs to *House & Garden, House Beautiful, Vogue, The New York Times Sunday Magazine, Time, Newsweek*, and other major magazines. Mr. Reens was born in Amsterdam, The Netherlands, and educated there and in France and Switzerland. With his wife, Anja, he now makes his home in Texas, but his assignments have taken him to Baghdad and Athens, to Germany, Haiti, Tunisia, and other parts of the world.

Romantic New Orleans

Text by DEIRDRE STANFORTH

Photographs by LOUIS REENS

PENGUIN BOOKS

For Tess Crager, whose urging brought this book to life

Penguin Books Ltd, Harmondsworth, Middlesex, England
Penguin Books, 625 Madison Avenue, New York, New York 10022, U.S.A.
Penguin Books Australia Ltd, Ringwood, Victoria, Australia
Penguin Books Canada Limited, 2801 John Street, Markham, Ontario, Canada L3R 1B4
Penguin Books (N.Z.) Ltd, 182–190 Wairau Road, Auckland 10, New Zealand

First published in the United States of America by The Viking Press 1977
Published in Penguin Books 1979

Text copyright © Deirdre Stanforth, 1977
Black-and-white photographs copyright © Louis Reens, 1977
Color photographs copyright in all countries of the International Copyright Union by
Louis Reens 1977
All rights reserved

LIBRARY OF CONGRESS CATALOGING IN PUBLICATION DATA
Stanforth, Deirdre.
Romantic New Orleans.
Reprint of the 1977 ed. published by The Viking Press,
New York, in series: A Studio book.
Includes index.
1. Historic buildings—Louisiana—New Orleans.
2. New Orleans—Buildings. 3. New Orleans—Description.
4. New Orleans—History. I. Reens, Louis. II. Title.
[F379.N58A27 1979]   976.3'35   78–10661
ISBN O 14 00.5058 2

Text and black-and-white photographs printed in the United States of
America by Halliday Lithograph Corporation, West Hanover, Massachusetts
Color illustrations printed in Japan by Dai Nippon Printing Company, Ltd., Tokyo
Set in Garamond

Acknowledgments

The preparation of this book would not have been possible without the advice, help, and cooperation of many people. Among those whose assistance we gratefully acknowledge are the following: Doris Antin, Albert Aschaffenburg, Blake Ashburner, Mrs. Bryan Bell, C. J. Blanda, Representative Lindy Boggs, Ella and Adelaide Brennan, David Campbell, Mrs. Kent Carruth, John Chase, Mrs. M. D. Claiborne, Mr. and Mrs. E. P. Crozat, Boyd Cruise, C. M. Davis, Mrs. Gerald Derks, Mr. and Mrs. J. D. Didier, Mr. and Mrs. Benjamin Erlanger, Mrs. F. Evans Farwell, Thomas Favrot, Muriel Francis, Stanton Frazar, Mr. and Mrs. Richard W. Freeman, Jr., Mrs. Eugene French, Vaughn Glasgow, Kari Guild, Mrs. Sheldon Hackney, Ann Haddow, Barbara Harvey, Rivet Hedderel, John Heim, Mrs. Sam Israel, Dr. Robert Judice, Thomas C. Keller, Henry Krotzer, Mrs. H. Merritt Lane, Mr. and Mrs. Isadore Lazarus, Don McCarter, Peggy McCloskey, Myra Menville, Dulaney Montgomery, Mary Elizabeth Pool, Mrs. Robert Potts, Mrs. Charles Reilly, Mr. and Mrs. Alan Rinehart, Martha Robinson, Mrs. Albert Ruhlman, Mrs. Joseph Schlosser, Mrs. Edgar B. Stern, Mrs. Frank Strachan, Anne R. Sutherlin, Mrs. R. Taggart, Michael Tarver, Dr. Nia Terezakis, Mrs. Clem Weston, Benjamin Yancey, and Mary Zervigon.

We would also like to express our appreciation to Seffi Rohregger, who made all the black-and-white prints; to Ehrenreich Photo-Optical Industries, Inc., for making available a 28-mm Nikkor P.C. lens before it was on the market; and to the staff of WDSU-TV, for their kindness in allowing us to use their reviewing stand to photograph the Mardi Gras parade. And we are grateful to editor Mary Velthoven and designer Chris Holme for their excellent work with our material.

Most particularly, we would like to thank Valora Spencer, who gave so generously of her time and knowledge acquired through her group tours of the Garden District; and Pat Phillips, whose newspaper feature on New Orleans homes has made her an encyclopedic source of information.

Photograph of Gallier Hall, page 41, courtesy of Gallier Hall

Contents

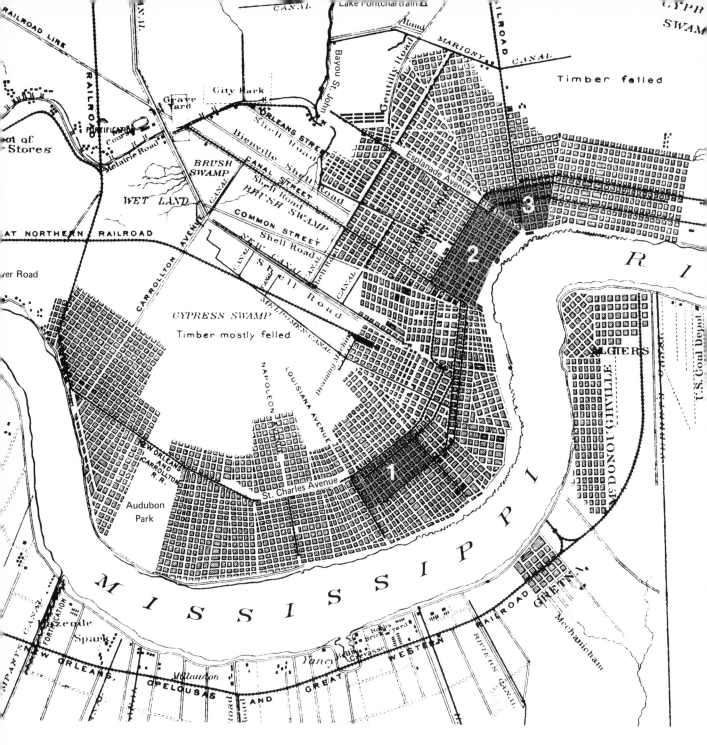

New Orleans. *Adaptation of a mid-nineteenth-century map.*
1. Garden District
2. French Quarter
3. Marigny

Building a City

No wonder New Orleans is different. Established for nearly a century as a European city before it became part of the United States, it took no part in the American Revolution, and its early settlers were certainly not Puritans. In spite of almost forty years of rule by Spain, its culture and language remained entirely French up to the time of the Louisiana Purchase in 1803—an event that was greeted with horror and hostility by its people, who looked upon Americans as barbarians.

The city's temperament, as well as its physical appearance, was molded in a crucible of cataclysms: its extreme tropical climate and the tempestuous Mississippi River drowned it in floods, hurricanes, and tornadoes; many of its buildings burned in countless fires, two of them major conflagrations; plagues of yellow fever and cholera repeatedly decimated its population; and financial panics and wars overturned its economic foundations. Because of this constant flirtation with death and disaster, in which the city's very existence was tested through successive trials, the Latin population developed an eat-drink-and-be-merry-for-tomorrow-you-may-die philosophy that is still noticeable today.

New Orleans is a curious mixture indeed. The city we see today evolved in three distinct phases. The original French city, now called either the Vieux Carré (old square) or the French Quarter, was entirely rebuilt during the period of Spanish rule, after a fire in 1788 had destroyed four-fifths of its buildings.

Following the Louisiana Purchase, Americans coming to New Orleans were so completely ostracized by the Creoles that they built their own city on the other side of Canal Street, and for a while New Orleans existed as two separate communities, living side by side in animosity. American society built its lavish homes in the Garden District, while Creole families vied with them by erecting their elegant houses up Esplanade Avenue on the other side of the French Quarter. The Americans built their own city hall on Lafayette Square, in the midst of the area that held their businesses, churches, and theaters. It was a city divided until the Americans at last prevailed through force of wealth and sheer numbers. The term "Dixie" originated in this period, when bilingual banknotes were printed with "10 dollars" on one side and the French "dix" on the other, and were nicknamed "dixies." Until the popular Civil War song made it a term denoting the entire South, only New Orleans was called Dixie.

The third New Orleans has been built in the years since World War II, after modern technology found a means of constructing skyscrapers in the city's soggy soil. Whether this is good or bad will not concern us here, for this book is about the qualities that make the city different, interesting, and picturesque, and not those that make it the same as other cities.

Though French, Spanish, and Anglo-Saxon were the major ingredients in the New Orleans melting pot, seasoning in the exotic stew included German, Italian, and a strong African influence. For not only did slaves make up a large part of the population, but free people of color, the *gens de couleur,* were also an important element in New Orleans, until the Civil War wiped out all class distinction among blacks. White families have always quailed at any implication of Negro blood, but young Creole gentlemen

customarily took beautiful quadroons as their mistresses, established them in houses of their own (often with slaves), provided for their futures, and fathered their children. Voodoo queen Marie Laveau was the product of such a union.

For more than two centuries ownership of this land on the North American continent was passed back and forth between France and Spain. Though first discovered by the Spanish in the sixteenth century, the Louisiana Territory was claimed for France by La Salle in 1682. Pierre le Moyne, sieur d'Iberville, was sent to colonize the territory, setting up his headquarters at Biloxi on the Gulf Coast. The site for New Orleans was chosen in 1718 by his brother, Jean Baptiste le Moyne, sieur de Bienville, who founded it as the capital of a vast French empire in the New World.

Bienville chose a location that was on the Mississippi River, but far enough removed from its mouth to be protected from the tropical storms and hurricanes that sweep in from the Gulf of Mexico. However, at that time, access up the river from the Gulf to the chosen site of the settlement was almost impossible. Not only was it difficult to navigate upstream against the current, but the mouth of the river was clogged with driftwood and debris and filled with treacherous sandbars. Bienville learned from the Indians of a safe and easy shortcut, a back-door route to his city on the river, from the Gulf via Lake Borgne and Lake Pontchartrain, through Bayou St. John. Here, at the curve of the Bayou, Bienville landed his men to begin clearing the swampy wilderness and establish the city of New Orleans. For a long time all sailing vessels landed at this port, which was connected to the city by an ancient Indian trail through the woods called the Grand Route St. John.

All great cities are based on rivers, and in placing this one near the mouth of a major American waterway, Bienville foresaw control of the commerce of half the continent. And in fact, that is precisely what happened until the advent of the railroad. But it was a love-hate relationship from the start; the city that was to reap such prosperity from the river spent many of its early years fighting to keep the Mississippi out. From the beginning there was a constant struggle against floods that inundated and washed out the settlement, leaving mud, snakes, crocodiles, and mosquitoes, which, in turn, brought yellow-fever plagues that were to torture the city for months at a time, year after year, throughout the nineteenth century. In spite of the earth levees that lined the river's banks, New Orleans was never safe from its temperamental rampages until the twentieth century, when a means was found to control it—a spillway built above the city that allows the swollen river to be released across undeveloped land into Lake Pontchartrain.

The first settlers of this quagmire were either brought by force or tricked into coming in exactly the same manner that people today are defrauded in sales of worthless land. To fill up the vast empty spaces of its Louisiana Territory after the supply of criminals and political refugees was exhausted, France devised the Mississippi Company and placed it in control of an imaginative and unscrupulous Scot, John Law. Law was inspired to heights of hucksterism that would put his contemporary counterparts to shame. Investment in Louisiana land was painted as a guarantee of wealth and happiness, the promise of a utopian future. Frenchmen (and later, Germans) were tempted by pictures of Indians pouring gold, silver, and pearls at the feet of settlers, who offered mere trinkets in exchange. New Orleans was depicted as a nirvana, a glorious land of ease and plenty. In fact, it was a crude, primitive settlement in a swampy wilderness, plagued by storms, searing tropical heat and humidity, insects, venomous reptiles, wild animals, and hostile Indians. Many of the deluded souls who sacrificed everything they owned to invest in this Godforsaken land never lived to see it. Those who survived the ocean voyage often perished on barren Massacre Island (later rechristened Dauphin Island by some early public-relations man) in Mobile Bay, where they were deposited without food or shelter to await transport to New Orleans in Bienville's boats.

The settlement did not develop into a glorious city overnight. The shortage of able-bodied men (and women), periodic flooding, and difficulties with the Indians, who wiped out Fort Rosalie upriver at

Bayou.

9

the site of Natchez and massacred two hundred and fifty colonists, made progress extremely slow and painful. And the combination of riffraff from French prisons and aristocratic political refugees made for a life of extreme contrasts as well as danger. Crime was rife, and punishment was harsh, brutal, and gory.

Bienville arrived with six ships, bringing six carpenters and thirty laborers. Primarily former convicts, they were undersized, unfit, and unwilling. Bienville wrote many letters home complaining of the inadequate work force he had been given. Nevertheless, a section of the swamp was cleared, and engineers Blond de la Tour and Adrien de Pauger laid out the city in a regular grid of streets around a central square that faced the river. Their plan and most of their street names remain in the Vieux Carré. Nearly a century later, when it became part of America, the entire city still consisted of only one hundred blocks. Everything beyond this cleared area was impenetrable swamp, except for the large plantation of Philippe de Marigny below the city, and a small settlement surrounding Bayou St. John, which was the city's port before the Mississippi became navigable. This landing area was connected to the new town two miles away by the Grand Route St. John. There is still a street by that name following the path of the oldest route into the city.

Drainage ditches surrounded each block, and they were so often filled with water that for many years blocks were known as "islets." The perimeter of the town was palisaded and moated, with forts at each corner—hence the name Rampart Street at the edge of the Vieux Carré. The first houses were crudely constructed of cypress slabs chinked with mud reinforced with Spanish moss, and roofed with palmetto thatch. There are puzzling contradictions in contemporary descriptions: while an Ursuline nun gives a glowing report, favorably comparing the city to Paris, another visitor in 1722 depicts "rude huts that would not grace a French village." However, this did not prevent wealthy colonists from filling their primitive dwellings with fine furnishings imported from France, or from ornamenting themselves with opulent, elaborate raiment.

In the early stages of the town's development a shipment of young women had to be sent over from France as wives for the settlers. They were called cas*ket* girls (with the accent on the last syllable, from *filles à la cassette*) because each was provided with a chest of clothing and linens as a dowry. In 1727 a group of Ursuline nuns arrived to look after the young women and to educate their offspring. The Ursuline Convent, constructed in 1734, is said to be the oldest building still standing in the Mississippi valley. Though this imposing edifice has an impressive French Renaissance exterior, its interior is severely simple. The diary of one of the nuns describes the city upon their arrival, following a perilous crossing:

> Our town is very handsome, well constructed and regularly built. . . . The streets are large and straight. The houses well built, with upright joists, the interstices filled with mortar, and the exterior whitewashed with lime. In the interior they are wainscoted. The roofs of the houses are covered with shingles which are cut in the shape of slates, and one must know this to believe it, for they all have the appearance and beauty of slate. . . . I do not, however, speak of the manners of the laity, but I am told that their habits are corrupt and scandalous. There are, however, a great number of honest people, and one does not see any of those girls who were said to have been deported on compulsion. . . . The women here are extremely ignorant as to the means of securing their salvation, but they are very expert in the art of displaying their beauty. There is so much luxury in this town that there is no distinction among the classes so far as dress goes. The magnificence of display is equal to all. Most of them reduce themselves and their family to a hard lot of living at home on nothing but sagamité [hominy cooked with meat or fish], and flaunt abroad in robes of velvet and damask, ornamented with the most costly ribbons. They paint and rouge to hide the ravages of time, and wear on their faces, as embellishment, small black patches.

Cypress swamp.

The exaggerated display of luxury in such a primitive environment became even more pronounced a few years later, in 1743, when Bienville was succeeded by a new colonial governor, Pierre Cavagnal de Rigaud, Marquis de Vaudreuil. The Marquis and his wife brought all the pomp and ostentatious elegance of the court at Versailles to the muddy streets of this frontier settlement in the midst of reptile-infested swamps. There followed a constant round of balls and banquets, featuring silks, satins, velvets, and lace; crystal and gold plate overflowed with fine wines and abundant food. The colonists loved it. The Marquis, who ruled for ten years, is remembered as one of New Orleans' most popular governors, when in fact the Vaudreuils set an early precedent for graft and corruption that was to become traditional in the city's later history. The Vaudreuils took money from the city treasury to deal in liquor and drugs, selling to the lazy, undisciplined soldiers and to blacks and Indians. This lax and venal administration encouraged the element of the population that had been dumped on the colony by the Mississippi Company, enhancing the settlement's already notorious reputation as a town of loose morals where murder and robbery were commonplace. In the taverns and gambling dens that began to proliferate along the riverfront and edges of the swamp, drinking, stealing, and whoring flourished.

Vaudreuil, promoted to the governorship of Canada, departed in a last blaze of glory, including fireworks, released doves, and a continuously flowing fountain of wine for the populace. His successor, a

Ursuline Convent on Chartres Street.   Lafitte's Blacksmith Shop.

navy captain, Louis Billouard de Kerlérec, striving vainly to restore honesty, discipline, and justice, earned a reputation for cruelty and brutality. Heartily detested by the citizens, he was recalled to Paris, judged on the basis of accusations by colonists, and exiled. The contrast between the popularity of these two governors says something about political preferences in the city of New Orleans.

Suddenly, in 1764, this French outpost in the New World was shocked to learn that it had been turned over to Spain by the King of France. At the end of the Seven Years' War, France had lost Canada and all of Louisiana east of the Mississippi except New Orleans. In a secret treaty Louis XV had given the remainder of Louisiana to his cousin Charles III of Spain. That was in 1762, but it was six years before the reluctant Spanish finally took possession of this gift.

The French citizens of New Orleans were so bitter about the ceding of their colony to a foreign power that a group of prominent men led a revolt against Don Antonio de Ulloa, who in 1766 had been sent by Spain to govern them. In 1768 Ulloa was expelled, and the ship on which he had taken refuge was driven out to sea. The rebellion was put down, and the leaders were executed in the public square by an Irishman in the service of Spain with the unforgettable name of Don Alexander O'Reilly. The Spanish governors who followed were far better administrators than their French predecessors.

Though Spain governed New Orleans for the remainder of the eighteenth century, it appears to have had little effect on the city's manners and customs. The Spanish influence was simply absorbed, becoming part of the total European atmosphere that prevailed, while language, customs, and mores

Street-side view of a garconnière.

remained steadfastly French. The entire city was rebuilt during this period. Ironically, the so-called French Quarter was constructed under Spanish rule. While Herbert Asbury in *The French Quarter* calls the resulting architecture completely Spanish, the distinguished nineteenth-century architect Benjamin Latrobe described it as "entirely French." In fact, there are elements of both, strongly influenced by native materials, the environment, and the subtropical climate.

Nothing remains of the primitive wooden town built by the first French settlers. Most of it was wiped out on Good Friday, 1788, by the fire that started in the home of Don José Vincente Nuñez, paymaster of the Spanish army. A candle on the altar of the chapel in his house at Chartres and Toulouse streets ignited the draperies, starting a conflagration that quickly spread while citizens were observing Good Friday. The refusal of the priests to ring the church bells on a holy day in order to spread the alarm resulted in the destruction of 856 buildings and the church. There is no record of how many houses were rebuilt in the next six years, before a second fire in 1794, which also occurred on a religious holiday, the Feast of the Immaculate Conception, demolished more than two hundred structures. Only two years after this second disastrous fire a frightful yellow-fever plague became the first of a series of epidemics that recurred throughout the nineteenth century, killing as many as six thousand people in one year.

With the slate wiped clean, the colonists began rebuilding their town, under an ordinance prohibiting wooden roofs. The first dwellings were based on European half-timbered construction. A framework of cypress timbers, braced with diagonal crossbeams, was filled in with native brick. This building method was called *briqueté entre poteaux* (bricked between posts). An example of it may be seen where patches of stucco have fallen off Lafitte's Blacksmith Shop in the 1100 block of Bourbon Street. Because the local brick was soft, porous, and absorbent, the surface was plastered over with stucco to weatherproof exterior walls, which were then painted a light color. Dwellings were usually one and a half stories, with a shop on the ground floor and bedrooms for the owner and his family upstairs under the gables. Roofs were low and steeply pitched, with a broad overhang projecting over the sidewalk. While there are a few of these small dwellings still scattered throughout the French Quarter (two rows of them on either side of Jackson Square were replaced by the Pontalba buildings), the majority of the buildings that give the old quarter its unique character are larger houses that were erected between 1800 and 1830.

As architect Nathaniel Cortlandt Curtis so aptly put it, in *New Orleans, Its Old Houses, Shops, and Public Buildings,* "social customs, local materials and cultured taste contributed to making these delightful dwellings almost personal witnesses of their environment." These later, larger houses were two to two and a half stories, with flat roofs, their simple façades built flush with the sidewalk. Since the poorly drained streets of the city alternated between disagreeable dust and seas of mud bordered by filthy gutters, the interior beauties of these houses were well-hidden and protected from the unpleasant outside world. A doorway in the front wall led through a long carriageway to an oasis of greenery in the rear that was completely walled, and removed from the noise and dirt of the street.

Design of these houses, based on the earliest Greek and Latin plans for tropical climates, used every possible means to take advantage of available shade and breezes. The main house and rear *garçonnière* (bachelor's quarters) were built around the open courtyard, with arched loggias, galleries, and long French doors that could be protected from the sun by louvered shutters. Like the earlier houses, they were built of native brick covered with stucco (since stone was not readily available), and the ground floor often contained shops or offices, with the main rooms of the house on the second floor. Rooms were beautifully proportioned, with high ceilings, handsome moldings, cornices and mantels, graceful curving stairways,

Bourbon Street.

French Quarter galleries.

and wide, arched fanlights over rear doorways. Architectural detail was simple, serving as a setting for elegant chandeliers, carpets, and furnishings imported from Europe. Exteriors of houses were always painted in light colors, with grayish-green woodwork. Ornamental iron balconies on the severely simple façades were at first made of wrought iron, and later of iron cast in much more elaborate patterns, at two local ironworks.

The streets of the old city centered on the public square, the Place d'Armes, on the bank of the Mississippi. It was originally a military parade ground, with a gallows in the center and, set along the sides, pillories for the punishment of minor infractions of the law. Here the flag of Spain was raised and leaders of the French rebellion executed by a firing squad. The town's first church stood in the center of the street facing the square, but it was destroyed, along with most other public buildings, in the fires of 1788 and 1794.

The buildings that line the square today, forming one of the most beautiful, symmetrical groupings in North America, are a monument to the city's greatest benefactor, Don Andres Almonaster y Roxas and his colorful daughter. This wealthy Andalusian nobleman contributed a long list of public buildings that were constructed immediately after the second fire; the most important and least altered being the Cabildo, or city hall, erected in 1795 to house "the Illustrious Cabildo," the Spanish governing body that had been set up in 1769 by Don Alexander O'Reilly to administer the colony. Don Almonaster himself was the architect, using more than a hundred of his own slaves and materials.

Le Prêtre house, Dauphine Street.

The Cabildo and (opposite) entrance gates.

It was in the Sala Capitular of the Cabildo in 1803 that official documents were signed that made New Orleans part of the United States. First the Spanish government returned the colony to delegates from France, and then, twenty days later, the French commissioner signed it over to America under the Louisiana Purchase, as negotiated by Thomas Jefferson. Thus, within three weeks, the flags of three nations were raised in the Place d'Armes outside the Cabildo.

Except for the mansard roof and dormer windows that were added in 1847, and a change of the sculpture in the pediment to an American motif after the Louisiana Purchase, the exterior appearance of the Cabildo has remained unchanged. During an extensive restoration in the 1960s, the missing mantel in the Sala Capitular was copied from an existing one of the period in the Bosque house, in an effort to restore this room to the way it looked in 1803. The purpose of the Cabildo changed from government palace, military headquarters and calaboose (jail), to city hall, to Louisiana State Museum, but the sublime sculptural mass of its exterior has continued to be a vital element in America's most beautiful city square. Its symmetry, and repetition of forms with variations, is rather like a visual fugue, as the rhythmic

18

OPPOSITE: The Cabildo, St. Louis Cathedral, and the Presbytère, facing Jackson Square.

OVERLEAF: Interior of St. Louis Cathedral (left) and Pirate's Alley (right).

Statue of Andrew Jackson.

colonnade of arches is repeated along the ground-floor entrance, and on the second story, with the addition of handsome fanlights, set off with the finest Spanish ironwork.

At the same time that the Cabildo was built, Don Almonaster gave the city a new cathedral, erected next door, on the site of the original church of St. Louis that had been leveled by fire. He is buried

21

in the cathedral, where a daily mass continues to be said in his honor, though the façade of his church has been modified to the point that he would no longer recognize it. Originally its design was more in keeping with the style of the Cabildo, but its bell-shaped towers were replaced by spires in a mid-nineteenth-century reconstruction. The Presbytère next to the cathedral was built about 1815 to match the Cabildo.

The name of the Place d'Armes was changed to Jackson Square in the mid-nineteenth century, when the city chose to honor Andrew Jackson, hero of the Battle of New Orleans. The square's equestrian statue of Jackson by Clark Mills, remarkable for its balance on the horse's rear legs, was one of three castings; the other two are in Nashville, Tennessee (Jackson's home), and in Lafayette Square, opposite the White House in Washington, D.C. The inscription on the base, "The Union must, and shall be preserved," was added during the Civil War by the despised Union general, Benjamin Butler.

The large, handsome red brick buildings flanking the other two sides of the square were added by Don Almonaster's flamboyant daughter, the Baroness Micaela de Pontalba, in 1850. When Don Almonaster was sixty years old, he had married Creole aristocrat Louise de la Ronde, who was young enough to be his daughter. Two girls were born to them, but only Micaela lived, and when her father died at seventy-three, she was still a baby. Her mother, a wealthy widow in her forties, married a young man of twenty-five. It was the custom in New Orleans to celebrate marriages with the barbarous clamor of a charivari, in which newlyweds were persecuted by a singing and shouting mob beating on pots and pans and ringing cowbells. The reaction to the marriage of Don Almonaster's middle-aged widow to such a young man caused a charivari that broke all records. It lasted for three days and nights, featured effigies of the new bridegroom, and Don Almonaster in a coffin, and did not cease until the bride promised a gift of three thousand dollars to the poor.

Though the city disapproved of this marriage, society was overjoyed at the match arranged for Micaela with Celestin, son of the wealthy, distinguished nobleman Baron de Pontalba. For more than a century the union of these two great families was considered the most important ever contracted in New Orleans, in spite of its unhappy consequences. Micaela was a fiery-tempered sixteen-year-old redhead. She was strong-willed and intelligent, but not a beauty (in fact, her face was described as resembling that of her horse). Her twenty-year-old bridegroom, a spoiled, petted youth, had the more feminine characteristics that she lacked—a soft, pretty face and delicate manners. Micaela, just completing her education in the Ursuline Convent, was in love with an impecunious youth, but as was customary, yielded to her mother's will in the arranged marriage, in a ceremony performed in St. Louis Cathedral by the beloved priest Père Antoine.

The newlyweds departed for France, accompanied by both their mothers, and went to live in the country, where they produced three children. Micaela soon became bored with family and country life. As soon as her mother died, leaving her the Almonaster fortune, she deserted husband and children for Paris. There she bought a magnificent mansion, gave entertainments attended by the *haut monde,* built a theater on the grounds, and acted in it herself. She became well-known for her lavish life-style, her fashionable clothes, and her lovers.

In October 1834, during a visit to the Pontalba country estate at Mont l'Evêque, an argument with her father-in-law over her scandalous behavior resulted in a bizarre duel. Though there were no witnesses, the sound of loud, angry voices was overheard. Shots rang out, followed by silence. When servants broke into the locked room, the eighty-year-old Baron was found, pistol in hand, with his brains spattered all over the Brussels carpet. Micaela, also clutching a gun, lay unconscious on the floor in a pool of blood, with bullets in her body and a finger shot off.

After recovering from her wounds, Micaela enjoyed another period of extravagant living in Paris as the Baroness de Pontalba. With revolution impending in France in 1848, she returned to the city of her birth to reign over New Orleans society. As a mature woman, she had become handsome as well as

Balcony ironwork displaying the monogram of the Baroness Pontalba.

elegant, and her soirées and salon were attended by everyone of importance. The New Orleans that Micaela found on her return was vastly changed from the European city she had known as a girl. When she had left, life had still centered around the Vieux Carré and plantation homes. Now French families were deserting the old quarter for new houses on Esplanade Avenue, and an American city was being created, with large, ornate homes rising in the uptown Garden District. Businesses and shops were moving from the French Quarter to the new American sector on the other side of Canal Street. The handsome square left by her father was becoming dingy; the Place d'Armes itself was overgrown with weeds, and the rows of small dwellings containing shops, cafés, and fruit stalls, built by Don Almonaster when he constructed the Cabildo and Cathedral, were now half deserted.

To remedy this situation, the Baroness resolved to demolish these outmoded buildings on either side of the square. Having wrung an agreement from the city for a twenty-year tax exemption, she hired an architect to design handsome new structures to flank the public buildings her father had erected. She first chose James Gallier, Jr., as architect, but he was soon replaced by Henry Howard. Doubtless the strong-willed Micaela proved a difficult, opinionated client. She herself designed the famous cast-ironwork that decorates the balconies, with her initials, A P (for Almonaster-Pontalba) in the center of each section. She also rode about daily, astride her horse, supervising work on the buildings, much of which was done by her own slaves. And while she appeared nightly at balls and parties elegantly gowned and coiffed as a great lady, by day she might be found climbing a ladder to the roof to inspect construction of her new buildings.

Although the handsome matching red brick Pontalba buildings have often been called the country's earliest apartments, they were actually rows of town houses, each with its own cooking wing, courtyard, and servants' quarters in the garret. Each row was designed as a unified blockfront, in the English fashion so popular in London and in the Georgian crescents and circles of Bath, presenting the appearance of one large building. There were many such buildings erected in New York at this period, but only half

Apartment bedroom in one of the Pontalba buildings shown opposite.

of one, Colonnade Row (1832), remains, and that in poor condition. The Pontalba buildings may be one of the rare existing American examples of this style of architecture.

There are conflicting stories about how much the Baroness had to do with changes in the square itself. Some say that she rechristened the Place d'Armes Jackson Square and chose to have a statue of Andrew Jackson erected in the center, contributing liberally to the fund for its creation. However, it is known that the Jackson Monument Association got the legislature to appropriate ten thousand dollars to commission the sculpture by Clark Mills, and it was unveiled in 1856, five years after the Baroness left for France. Reportedly the square was landscaped after the monument was dedicated, but there is a contrary and far more dramatic story—that the fiery Baroness, having laid out the circular paths and gardens for the park in front of her new buildings, faced down the Mayor with a shotgun when he tried to stop her from felling the double row of trees that stood on either side of the square.

In any case, her new buildings surely inspired refurbishing of the square, as well as enhanced her father's contribution by completing the beautifully balanced architectural composition of its three sides. Also, for a time at least, she succeeded in attracting the return of aristocratic families to the heart of the old quarter. The town houses of the Pontalba buildings, as elegant and fashionable as any in the city, were the setting for the entertainment of society and visiting celebrities. When the Swedish Nightingale, Jenny Lind, came to the city to perform, Micaela turned over to her the central house that had been handsomely furnished for her own use, and also gave her a fine chef, Boudro, to serve her. When the singer departed, her farewell speech expressed her deepest gratitude to the Baroness and Boudro.

26

Creole Society and Plantation Life

As illustrated by the union of Don Almonaster y Roxas and Louise de la Ronde, intermarriage between French and Spanish was soon accepted in New Orleans, in spite of the colony's bitterness at being ruled by Spain. The children of these marriages were called Creoles. The word "Creole" was derived from the Spanish *criollo* (its root in the verb *criar,* to create, or breed) to designate the offspring of Europeans that were born in the colonies. Though the word itself was of Spanish derivation, it soon came to have primarily French implications. It is fascinating to note the overpowering influence of the French language, culture, and civilization in this New World outpost. Repeatedly outnumbered and intermarried, the French still managed to remain dominant in name, taste, and temperament well into the twentieth century, absorbing Spanish, German, and even American influences. When Spain took over New Orleans, there were only five thousand inhabitants, one third of whom were slaves. The population doubled under Spanish rule and quadrupled in the first decade after the Purchase, and yet this tiny proportion of the city's inhabitants continued to make its influence felt.

When French married Germans, not only were offspring given French first names but in no time even German surnames were translated or bastardized into French. Zweig became LaBranche, Farber became Fabre, and Jake Schneider was transformed into the Creole name of Schexnaydre! Even the streets named after the nine muses, in the American sector of the city, are today universally mispronounced in anglicized French.

Though the word "Creole" was often extended to refer to possessions, including "Creole slaves," and therefore became misunderstood as referring to blacks or mulattoes, in fact the Creoles were (and still are) as conscious and careful of their bloodlines as royalty. In their zeal to guard against what they regard as disastrous marriages, they have always been able to recite the entire family tree of any of their compatriots. So often did cousins intermarry that some say all Creoles are related.

Family, pride, and honor were always paramount, followed by manners, culture, breeding, and taste. All Creoles were Catholic; in the Black Code of 1724 Bienville had expressly forbidden the practice of any other religion. All Jews were excluded, and while Protestants were tolerated, they were not allowed to hold religious services. Until the Louisiana Purchase brought religious freedom and the building of Protestant churches, services were held in secret in private homes. The Creoles took their religion very seriously but never allowed it to interfere with their inherent *joie de vivre.* They always went to Mass on Sunday morning, but the rest of the day was given over to shopping, visiting, matinees, and supper parties. The celebration of Mardi Gras epitomizes their attitude toward life and religion. "Mardi Gras," the "Fat Tuesday" preceding Ash Wednesday, is the last day before the fasting of Lent. Creoles turned the approach of this austere religious observance into an occasion for an almost pagan orgy that goes on for months before a relatively brief Lenten solemnity, which is not taken too seriously. Work has never been regarded as anything but a necessary evil. Among the early Creoles, a well-born young man with no money was simply expected to make a good marriage with a wealthy lady. Money was never considered of primary importance; it was not what one did but whom one was descended from that counted—and still does today. There is a joke that the Creoles are like the Chinese—they eat rice and worship their ancestors.

No Creole ever worked with his hands; wealth was acquired through the labor of slaves on the vast acreage of plantation lands lining the Mississippi for a hundred miles. And huge fortunes were made from lumber, rice, tobacco, indigo, cotton, and sugar. One of the richest Creole families, the Bringiers, owned most of the plantations, and various Bringier relatives built homes like Hermitage and Tezcuco along the River Road in varying degrees of splendor.

The famous Southern hospitality was lavished on guests, who arrived in droves, often staying for weeks at a time—one is reported to have remained for twenty-seven years! Families moved their entire households back and forth between plantations in the summer and New Orleans town houses in the winter. Life in the city centered in balls, theater, and opera. Almost nightly, gay and glittering affairs were attended by Creole society in an atmosphere of extreme contrast. Slaves led the way with lanterns through dark, muddy streets lined with foul-smelling open ditches filled with sewage and garbage, often skirting the corpses of murder victims along the way. At the ballroom entrance the slaves washed the mud off their mistresses' feet and reshod them in silk stockings and satin dancing slippers before the ladies were ushered in on the arms of gentlemen handsomely clad in evening clothes.

Gentlemen had an absolute obligation to defend their honor against any imagined slight or insult, and so many fights erupted among men attending these balls that the wearing of swords finally had to be prohibited. On one occasion a battle was started by a dispute over the music to be played by the orchestra. Challenges were flung down on the most trivial provocation, followed by duels fought either in St. Anthony's garden behind the St. Louis Cathedral or under the oaks on the Allard plantation, now City Park. There were several fencing masters (colorful characters all) who were kept busy teaching young men to defend themselves. One, Pepé Llulla, was said to have had his own cemetery for the unfortunate losers. In any case, the St. Louis cemeteries are full of dueling victims, whose epitaphs indicate that they died on the field of honor.

Opera was very important in the life of Creole New Orleans. The first regular performances of grand opera in America were presented in New Orleans a decade before they began in New York, and the great diva Adelina Patti was presented in the Vieux Carré in 1853, long before her New York debut. Families attended the opera several nights a week; it was imperative for anyone of importance to be seen there on Tuesday and Saturday evenings. Daughters were introduced to society in the boxes of the opera house, where eligible young men called upon them during intermissions.

There was a series of fine opera houses built in the French Quarter, the last, grandest, and most important having been the French Opera House, on Bourbon and Toulouse streets. Designed and built by architect James Gallier, Jr., in 1859, in the incredibly short period of six months, it was described by the *New Orleans Delta* as "a truly magnificent theatre": that rose "like a Colossus over everything in the vicinity," with seating for eighteen hundred, seven elegant stores in the basement, and cafés on either corner. When the building burned down in 1919, writer Lyle Saxon summed it up in the *Times-Picayune* as the end of an era: "The heart of the French Quarter stopped beating last night." No opera house was ever built to replace it, and as the Creole influence began to decline, so did the culture of New Orleans. Where there were once several opera houses and theaters for performances by companies of international renown, and a number of American theaters following the Creole example, the city went through a large part of the twentieth century with no professional theaters at all.

Gambling was a major recreation of Creole men. Bernard de Marigny lost his family's vast fortune largely through his passion for gambling, eventually having to subdivide the Marigny plantation and sell off lots in the area now known as the Faubourg Marigny. Marigny was the personification of Creole ideals. By American standards, he ended a ruined man, a failure. But Grace King, presenting the Creole point of view (in *Old Families of New Orleans*) describes him thus:

. . . the hero *par excellence* of New Orleans' social traditions. . . . He, more than any of his family or men of his time, is responsible for what we call today the Creole type; originating the standard of fine living and generous spending, of lordly pleasure and haughty indifference to the cost; the standard which he maintained so brilliantly for a half century, until even today, one receives, as an accepted fact, that not to be fond of good eating and drinking, of card playing and pretty ladies; not to be a *fin gourmet,* not to be sensitive about honor, and to possess courage beyond all need of proof is, in sober truth, if such a truth can be called sober—not to be a Creole.

It was a standard that required the greatest fortune Louisiana could produce to maintain it. It ravaged the great wealth of Marigny himself, and ruined many and many of the old families who tried to follow in his aristocratic footprints and who arrived at poverty as Bernard did but without the prestige that distinguished him to the end.

Bernard's father, Pierre Philippe de Marigny de Mandeville, had developed the enormous family fortune, adding vast lands granted for his service to Spain to the holdings already acquired by his father, who had served under Bienville. While still a youth, Philippe was the wealthiest man and largest landholder in Louisiana. Already the owner of a large plantation below the city, he bought plantations above New Orleans and across Lake Pontchartrain as well, where he acquired an extensive tract of forest. There he built a summer home, called Fontainebleau, surrounded by magnificent gardens and pine woods. Both this house and his home on the Marigny plantation in New Orleans were in the typical Louisiana style: large houses built on brick pillars, surrounded by broad galleries, whose turned-wood colonnettes supported a large hipped roof with dormer windows (Because of dampness, floods, snakes and other crawling creatures, it was customary to build houses on pilings or brick columns, as much as eight feet off the ground. This architectural style came to be known as "raised cottage," no matter how large or magnificent the house.) Philippe's plantation homes, like the Vieux Carré town houses, were very simply designed but elaborately decorated with luxurious furniture, Oriental rugs and fine carpets, paintings, *objets d'art,* crystal, china, and tableware imported from France. The lavish entertaining that took place in the Marigny homes reached its epitome in 1798, during the three-month visit of the royal princes of France, one of whom would become King Louis Philippe. There were balls and banquets, where sumptuous meals were served on gold plate, which was often tossed casually into the Mississippi River after one use, while cigars were lighted with hundred-dollar bills. When the future King departed, his host gave him an enormous loan, which was never to be repaid. Two years later, in 1800, Philippe de Marigny died, leaving his fifteen-year-old son, Bernard, heir to an estate exceeding seven million dollars. Before Bernard was eighteen, his guardian sent the spoiled, wild, extravagant youth abroad, where he became a friend of Lord Byron. Bernard reached his majority and returned to New Orleans to inherit his fortune in 1803, as the French were turning the Louisiana colony over to the Americans. After entertaining the French commissioner in a style surpassing his father's, Bernard was appointed to the staff of the new American government and became involved in politics. Following a brief marriage that ended with his wife's death, he began the courtship of his second wife, whom he met at a ball. Rivalry over the lady's favor at the ball led to seven challenges, all of which Marigny accepted, on condition that the duels be fought on seven consecutive mornings before breakfast. After he killed the first challenger with one thrust, the other six declined to meet him. Though he won the lady, the marriage was an unhappy one.

Marigny was elected to the State legislature and led the committee that met Andrew Jackson when he arrived to lead the city's defense against the British in the Battle of New Orleans. When Lafayette visited the city, he was entertained at Marigny's house in the usual princely fashion. A description (by Grace King in *Old Families of New Orleans*) of the repasts at the Marigny country estate at Fontainebleau give an indication of what that style of entertainment was like. It included "turkeys fattened on pecans; terrapin from his own pens; soft-shell crabs from the beach; oysters fresh from his own reefs; green

Dueling oak in City Park.

trout and perch from the bayous; sheepshead and croakers from the lake; pompano, red fish and snappers from the Gulf; vegetables from his own garden; cress from his own sparkling forest spring; fruit from his orchard; eggs, chickens, capons from his own fowl yard . . . with sherry, Madeira, champagne and liqueurs . . . combined in menus that Brillat-Savarin would have been glad to have composed." Bernard de Marigny once won a ten-thousand-dollar bet with a guest that he could serve an entire meal consisting only of ingredients from his own property. It is easy to see how he won the wager.

Balls, banquets, lavish entertainment, exquisite furnishings, and fine art were but minor extravagances compared to Marigny's passion for gambling. Gambling was a favorite occupation among Creole gentleman, but Bernard de Marigny was its most devoted adherent, often losing as much as thirty thousand dollars in an evening. The dice game called craps was introduced to America (perhaps by Louis Philippe, future King of France) at a house on the Marigny plantation. When his property later became the Faubourg Marigny, he named one of the streets Rue de Craps, after his favorite game. The street name later had to be changed to Burgundy when it became an embarrassment, particularly to a place of worship that became known as "the Craps Methodist Church."

In 1830 Bernard de Marigny and his son were guests of King Louis Philippe of France, who repaid the lavish Marigny hospitality, though not the loan. The King's gift to Bernard was a silver service, each piece of which was adorned with a portrait of the royal family. Bernard treasured this gift the rest of his life, but after his death it was sold by weight to the Mint to be melted down.

Though the family name was not perpetuated into present-day New Orleans by a male heir, Bernard gave the name of Mandeville to a town he created and laid out adjacent to his estate at Fontainebleau, and later, as his seven-million-dollar fortune dwindled to less than a million, he divided up the Marigny plantation into streets and lots for development, in the section of New Orleans now known as the Faubourg Marigny. He decided to make his own "Creole city" after a proposed sale of the property to the American entrepreneurs Peters and Caldwell collapsed when Madame de Marigny failed to appear at the contract signing.

The last remnant of the great Marigny fortune disappeared when two successive years of crop failures due to levee breaks, coupled with a crippling tariff on sugar, drove a hundred and thirty-six plantations (including two of Marigny's) into bankruptcy. Bernard de Marigny, who had lived with vast wealth under French, Spanish, and American rule, spent the remainder of his long life in a two-room apartment with one servant. But in typical Creole fashion, he maintained his pride, his sense of position, and his princely manner, reminiscing about duels he had fought, and visits with the King of France, Lafayette, Andrew Jackson, Henry Clay, and Sam Houston. He never forgot who he was, and neither did anyone else. When he walked too far from home and had to take an omnibus, the drivers would never accept a fare from the man who had once owned the land their routes traversed. When he died at the age of eighty-three, his obituary mourned "the last of the Creole aristocracy . . . one who knew how to dispose of a great fortune with contemptuous indifference."

Although the splendors of plantation life are now a thing of the past, some of the beautiful houses remain along the River Road above New Orleans: among them the Hermitage, Houmas, Tezcuco, and, diminished but still bravely holding its own, Elmwood, which now serves as a restaurant.

The Hermitage is one of the earliest Greek Revival homes in Louisiana. The plantation land was bought by Marius Pons Bringier in 1804, and given to his son Michel Doradou Bringier, who began building the house after his marriage to Aglae du Bourg in 1812. Shortly after its completion, Michel served under Andrew Jackson's command in the Battle of New Orleans, and so he named his plantation after Jackson's Tennessee home. General and Mrs. Jackson visited Bringier's Hermitage on their way back to Nashville from New Orleans.

Originally planted in indigo, its crop was later changed to sugar cane, and the plantation was equipped with its own sugar mill. The Bringier family either owned or married into some forty of the pre–Civil War plantations along the River Road, and when Michel Bringier died in 1847, his estate was worth $1.7 million, which was a vast fortune in the nineteenth century.

During the Civil War the Hermitage was confiscated, then leased to a carpetbagger. Despite severe devastation, it was rehabilitated and put back in operation by the Bringier family for a few more years following the Reconstruction period. However, the house was later abandoned and left to deteriorate for fifteen years. Fortunately, it was rescued by the present owner. It is one of the handful remaining of more than a hundred plantation houses that once stood along the Mississippi above New Orleans.

Dr. Robert Judice bought the Hermitage in 1959 and began a careful restoration, replacing lost pieces of woodwork with parts salvaged from other old houses in the area. The four rooms on each of the two floors, divided by a central hall, are decorated with appropriate Louisiana furnishings of the period. The simplicity of the interior, so typical of early plantations and French Quarter homes, may come as a surprise to many people, who associate the rows of huge white columns with opulence and grandeur. Though the Hermitage is a home, not a museum, it is shown by appointment on special tours, for which arrangements may be made by writing to Dr. Judice at 1323 Eighth Street, New Orleans, 70115.

The beautiful Greek Revival house of Houmas Plantation stands on land purchased from the chief of the Bayou Goula and Houmas Indians in 1774. This transaction, involving the sale of 14,000 fertile acres for $150, was almost as outrageous as the sale of Manhattan Island for $24. The original tract was later expanded to nearly 200,000 acres under Spanish land grants.

The Hermitage.

A room in the Hermitage.

ABOVE: Houmas Plantation. LEFT: A *pigeonnier* on the grounds. OPPOSITE, ABOVE: A parlor. OPPOSITE, BELOW: Kitchen at the rear of the house.

Tezcuco.

Elmwood.

At some time between 1775 and 1800, Alexander Latile, one of the two men who bought the land from the Indians, built a small French country house. This was later to be incorporated into the rear of the handsome Greek Revival structure. The property then changed hands several times, expanding and dwindling by turns; at one point it was divided into three separate plantations. In 1816 General Wade Hampton, an eminent and wealthy South Carolinian, bought it and restored the estate to its original size. After the General died in 1835, his land and 489 slaves were divided among his wife and daughters. Though the exact date is unknown, the splendid Houmas house was built by General Hampton's family sometime between 1830 and 1840. For the next decade it was the home of Hampton's daughter and son-in-law, Mr. and Mrs. John S. Preston, who also kept a town house in New Orleans. In 1858 the

36

Prestons sold the plantation to Irish immigrant John Burnside, who came to be known as the Sugar Prince, for $750,000.

While living at Houmas house, Burnside established a vast sugar refinery and gave his name to the nearby town. Burnside, a bachelor, willed his large fortune and the estate to his best friend, Oliver Bierne. The plantation and its sugar production were carried on by Bierne's son-in-law, William Porcher Miles. Miles culminated a widely diversified career as a mathematics professor, mayor of Charleston, South Carolina, and colonel on Beauregard's staff during the Civil War, by becoming a highly successful sugar manufacturer. After his death in 1899 his son, Dr. William P. Miles, Jr., abandoned a medical career to carry on the plantation and refinery. Following the failure of the sugar industry, the refinery closed down in 1912, and cultivation of sugar on the Miles company's thirteen plantations came to an end. Dr. Miles died in 1935, and in 1940 his widow sold Houmas to Dr. George Crozat.

Crozat, like Burnside, was a bachelor, and like Miles and the owners of nearby Hermitage and Tezcuco, a doctor—New Orleans' leading orthodontist. Restoration of the house and grounds became his passion. He called it his "ten-year project," but when he died twenty-six years later in 1966, he was still working on it. Left to his sisters, nieces, and nephew, Houmas Plantation was opened to the public in 1970. The shining white columns of the beautifully proportioned house, its authentically furnished interior, and its enchanting subsidiary buildings set in vast green lawns shaded by immense oak trees give tangible evidence of the way of life in a vanished era.

Although its rooms have very high ceilings and exceptionally wide Greek ear moldings, Tezcuco is a smaller-scale dwelling than nearby Houmas and Hermitage. It was one of the numerous plantation homes built and occupied by the Bringier family; the founder of this prolific dynasty, Maurice Pons Bringier, came from Provence, France, to Louisiana and established an extensive plantation in 1790. His sons and grandsons, daughters and granddaughters built homes along the River Road; cousins married cousins, and built still more, so that most of the houses still standing in the vicinity are connected in some way with the Bringier family.

Maurice Bringier's grandson Benjamin built Tezcuco in 1855, after marrying his cousin Aglae, daughter of Michel Doradou Bringier, who lived at nearby Hermitage Plantation. The house was named after a village on Lake Tezcuco, Montezuma's refuge, or resting place, in his flight from Cortez. The bed of the lake, Texcoco (the Spanish spelling of the Aztec name), became the site of Mexico City.

Though Tezcuco is open to the public, it is the full-time home of Dr. and Mrs. Robert Potts. Dr. Potts, who wanted to be a country doctor, exchanged his New Orleans home for Tezcuco. In spite of a demanding medical practice, he has found time to make beautiful photographs of Louisiana swamps and to carve miniature reproductions of the Potts collection of furniture by the famous New Orleans cabinetmakers Prudent Mallard and François Seignouret for a dollhouse displayed in this raised cottage.

Elmwood, one of the oldest Louisiana plantations, was probably built in the middle of the eighteenth century by Nicolas Chauvin de Lafrénière, who was executed in 1769 for leading the rebellion of French colonists against Governor Ulloa when New Orleans was ceded to Spain. It is known that the house existed in 1768; it was described in documents accompanying an act of sale in January of that year. Gun slots in the wall of a ground-floor room indicate that Indian attacks were still feared when the building was constructed.

The property changed hands many times. Its operation as a sugar plantation continued throughout the nineteenth century, when its outbuildings included a large sugar house, a steam-engine sugar mill, overseer's house, cook house, and blacksmith shop. The land was eventually acquired by the Illinois Central Railroad, and the house was left vacant and deteriorating. Though the railroad management refused to sell the property, they agreed to lease the decaying house to Mr. and Mrs. Jack Lemann in the 1920s, provided they restore the ancient oak trees as well as the house. The Lemanns, who found the fine Colonial plantation house a squalid wreck overrun with chickens, accomplished an extensive restoration. Unfortunately, they lived there only ten years, and sometime after they left, in 1940, a fire completely destroyed the second story, with its high, hipped roof, triple dormer windows, and wide galleries surrounded with turned-wood colonnettes. All that remained was the ground floor and its plastered brick Tuscan columns. A roof similar to the original was built on this lower story, but sadly, what is left of Elmwood is less than half of this beautiful eighteenth-century example of an early Louisiana raised cottage-style plantation house.

In 1961 Elmwood Plantation began a new life when chef Nick Mosca, whose family owns a popular restaurant, decided to open one of his own. So the two-century-old house, on its tree-shaded grounds behind the levee on the River Road, has become the setting for Italian-flavored Creole dining.

The Americans and the Garden District

Prior to the Louisiana Purchase in 1803, the only Americans known to the cultured, civilized citizens of the French-Spanish city were uncouth flatboatmen, called "Kaintucks" regardless of which state they came from. Bienville's dream had materialized. Transportation of freight overland across the mountains to the East Coast was so difficult that all merchandise was carried down the Mississippi River from St. Louis to New Orleans, to be either sold or loaded on ocean-going vessels to be shipped to other ports. All sorts of floating vehicles were used, but the most prevalent were huge keelboats or flatboats, great barges similar to arks. These vessels were carried downstream only by the current, with a giant oar called a broadhorn used to steer them off sand- or mudbanks. Keelboats could be propelled back upstream by sheer muscle power, with the crew towing or poling them against the river bottom, but it was a backbreaking journey of three to five months. Flatboats, with no means of making the return trip upriver, were simply broken up, and their timbers used as *banquettes* (sidewalks) or in the construction of houses. The crews had to journey north again on foot or on shared horses, in relays, up the dangerous route of the Natchez trace, the notorious hunting ground of murderous, cutthroat gangs of bandits.

The rough, tough flatboatmen led a rugged existence, living without shelter, on enormous quantities of whiskey and on bread and meat eaten from a communal pot. When they were not fighting off river pirates, they fought each other, terrorizing the populace with their brutal, bloody brawls. Each boat had its champion, who wore a red turkey feather in his hair or cap, representing a challenge to the physical prowess of every other passing boatman. The challenge was seldom refused, and the ensuing battles were fearsome and ferocious, including biting, kicking, stamping, gouging, clubbing, and any other means of mutilation.

Among flatboat heroes were several men—and a woman, Annie Christmas, who stood six feet eight inches tall and weighed two hundred and fifty pounds. She worked as a stevedore and on flatboats, and whipped every bully on the river. Among her legendary feats of strength was towing a loaded keelboat singlehanded from New Orleans to Natchez so fast that the boat skimmed over the water. For a change of pace, she dressed in female attire and became the madam of a floating brothel, where her escapades were equally unbelievable. Hers was one of a number of flatboats tied up in the port at New Orleans serving as bordellos and low drinking dives. The Kaintucks started their rampages on the waterfront prior to enjoying the further pleasures of a city that was famous for its sin. The police were helpless to control the binges of these wild Americans, and their invasions struck fear into the hearts of the sophisticated population.

Small wonder, then, that the Creoles were appalled to find their city suddenly ceded back from Spain to France and then immediately sold lock, stock, and barrel to the Americans! The Americans, flooding into the city whose port was second in the nation, and intent on settling down to make their fortunes, found the Creoles as strange as the Creoles found them. To the serious, hard-working Americans, the Creoles appeared frivolous, snobbish, and lazy. The puritanical Protestant Anglo-Saxons were mystified at the social promenading, cavorting, shopping, and theater-going of these Latin Catholics after Sunday morning Mass. And while the Creoles soon learned that all Americans were not as savage and revolting as the Kaintucks, they regarded them as uncivilized, ill-mannered, and crassly commercial, and certainly would not admit them into their exclusive, cultured society.

So the Americans proceeded to build their own city, in what was called the Faubourg Ste. Marie, on the other side of Canal Street. Lafayette Square replaced Jackson Square, and as a substitute for the Cabildo, the Americans built their own city hall. A complete departure from the Vieux Carré architecture, it was a massive example of the Greek Revival style that would become the prevailing theme of the new city. (Although since replaced by a new city hall, it still stands as Gallier Hall, named after its architect, James Gallier, Sr.) They erected their own churches, theaters, and hotels, and elegant homes began to rise along Canal Street (the only one remaining intact houses the prestigious Boston Club) and in the area just above today's Lee Circle. In order to break the political power of the Creoles, Americans rigged legislation that divided New Orleans into three separate cities. Before very long, the industrious Americans had gained the upper hand, as the city prospered and its population doubled and quadrupled.

In 1813 the distinguished architect Benjamin Latrobe was brought to New Orleans to design and build a *"Pompe à Feu"* to draw Mississippi River water into the city to sluice the gutters. And in 1821, under Creole Mayor Roffignac, the streets were paved for the first time, with large, diagonally laid blocks of granite from ships' ballast, and sidewalks of random pink and gray flagstones. Street lighting was introduced in the form of lanterns hung from posts at each intersection.

Ever imitating and vying with the Creoles, the Americans opened their first theater, in the midst of a swamp on Camp Street, just above Canal. It was the first building to be lit by gas. The audience was compelled to approach wearing boots, or along a narrow walk of flatboat timbers laid over the mud. The first large hotels in the United States were the Creole St. Louis Hotel, built in 1836, followed by the American St. Charles Hotel, in 1837. The St. Louis, a splendid edifice in the Classical Revival style which occupied the site of the Royal Orleans, was the architectural masterpiece of J. N. B. de Pouilly. Its magnificent dome, built in a method seen in the early Christian churches of Ravenna but unused for fourteen hundred years, had a shell constructed of an earthenware honeycomb, making it light enough to be supported by the city's wet soil. Its interior, decorated with murals by Dominique Canova, featured arches and colonnades and a grand spiral staircase. The rotunda was used as a merchants' exchange, where planters came to barter cotton, sugar, and slaves. From 1874 to 1877 the hotel served as the Louisiana State House, before the capital was moved to Baton Rouge.

On the other side of Canal Street stood the American St. Charles Hotel, designed by Gallier and Dakin, its classical portico approached by a flight of marble steps. Visitors compared it to St. Peter's in Rome and to the Czar's palace in St. Petersburg. On the other hand, Frederick Law Olmsted, co-designer of New York's Central Park, described it as "the great Grecian portico of the stupendous, tasteless, ill-contrived and inconvenient St. Charles Hotel." It also boasted a spiral staircase and a majestic dome circled with Ionic columns, and it was famed for its gold service, used for especially important dinners. The St. Charles, twice rebuilt after being severely damaged by fires, was demolished in the middle of the twentieth century.

The homes of Americans spread farther uptown, and an especially fine and fashionable section was built around Coliseum Square. This park was not really square but shaped rather like the Roman forum. In the zeal for classic revival, there was a plan to build a prytaneum there. Although the prytaneum never materialized, there is a street named Prytania, with cross streets named for the nine muses. The Coliseum Square area suffered a long period of deterioration but is now being restored.

Gallier Hall.

Statue of General Robert E. Lee in Lee Circle.

Sacred Heart Academy.   St. Mary's Dominican College.

The next American residential section developed along the river, outside the limits of the city at that time. Today it is called the Garden District; then it was the city of Lafayette, and prior to 1825 it was the Livaudais plantation. The lands above the business district of New Orleans were originally several large plantations, planted in sugar cane and indigo. In 1816 a crevasse appeared in the levee upriver at

the Macarty plantation, and the resulting flood of Mississippi River water deposited a layer of rich silt over this entire area, ruining crops but greatly increasing the fertility of its already rich soil.

One of the large plantations on the river, four miles above the city, was owned by the Livaudais family. A highly suitable match was arranged between the Livaudais's son and heir, François, and Céleste

The oldest (c. 1854) house on lower St. Charles Avenue.
It was designed by James Gallier, Sr.

de Marigny, sister of Bernard and daughter of Philippe de Marigny, the wealthiest man in Louisiana and perhaps in all America. François and his bride began building a large home on the Livaudais plantation, but it was left uncompleted when they separated in 1825. Céleste acquired the plantation as part of the settlement, and as she departed for a life at the court of the French King, she sold off the land for $500,-000, retaining only the unfinished house and the grounds around it. As the lots were sold for development, the unfinished house remained vacant. At one point it was used as a public ballroom and for a short time as a plaster factory. It had become known as "the haunted house" and was sheltering a few homeless derelicts when it was finally demolished in 1863.

The Livaudais land, which was to become the Garden District, was consolidated with four adjacent plantations into three communities, called Nuns, Lafayette, and Livaudais. In 1833 these three communities incorporated to become the city of Lafayette, and it was not until 1852 that Lafayette became part of the city of New Orleans. During its two decades Lafayette's riverfront was a busy port where cattle were unloaded at a slaughterhouse surrounded by tanneries, tallow and soap makers, hide merchants, and bone grinders. There was a grain elevator on the waterfront, and an area set aside for breaking up flatboats after they had unloaded their cargoes. Their long timbers were then used in the construction of cottages that were springing up on streets nearest the river, as well as for *banquettes*. Lafayette devoted one square block to its own cemetery, the American counterpart to the Creole cemeteries bordering the Vieux Carré.

Home of Mr. and Mrs. Ralph Scott Taggart
on Seventh Street.

Double-tiered portico of the home of Mr. and
Mrs. Frank Strachan at 1134 First Street. Jefferson Davis, President of the Confederacy,
died here.

Built in 1856 and 1857 as a residence for a Miss Lavinia Dabney, the former Archbishopric of the Episcopal Diocese is again a private home.

St. Charles Avenue streetcar.

Soulé College on Jackson Avenue was originally a private home. BELOW: A detail of the portico.

Cast-iron galleries of the Carroll-Crawford house at 1315 First Street match those of the Sam Israel house shown on page 55. Both were built in 1869.

Regular transportation was provided to the city of Lafayette from the American city downtown in the Faubourg Ste. Marie by horse-drawn, double-decker omnibus, and later by steam railroad (since supplanted by the streetcar) up St. Charles Avenue to the city of Carrollton, which had its own Greek Revival city hall, now serving as a high school. Prospering American businessmen seized the opportunity to buy lots on the Livaudais plantation to build homes in this fashionable new suburb.

The Americans, spurning the simple lines of the Creole homes, built elaborate mansions. Most had the newly popular Greek Revival façades, ornamented with local cast-ironwork. Their fluted columns were made of wood, but the buildings themselves were usually brick. However, the brick was never left exposed. Even though it no longer needed weatherproofing, it was always either painted or stuccoed and then painted. Often the stucco was scored to resemble stone. Interiors were embellished with plaster ceiling medallions and cornices, as well as carved marble mantels. Unlike Creole homes, these houses were set back from the street on large plots of land. Some, since demolished, occupied entire blocks. The fertile soil, enriched by silt from the floods which broke through the Macarty crevasse, encouraged the growth of trees, shrubs, and flowers that normally thrive in the wet tropical climate. (If everyone in the city were to cease controlling the rapid growth of foliage, New Orleans might completely disappear into the jungle within a decade!) The lordly new homes, their fluted columns painted in pale, muted tones, were soon surrounded by oaks, magnolias, banana and palm trees, crape myrtle, oleander, sweet olive, camellias, azaleas, bougainvillea, rosa-de-montana, wisteria, and roses.

One of the more famous residents of the Garden District was George Washington Cable. Although Cable was hailed as a genius elsewhere, and his *Old Creole Days, The Creoles of Louisiana,* and many books of short stories were widely acclaimed, he was thoroughly despised in New Orleans for writing them. The Creoles so detested Cable's depiction of them that he was cursed, publicly denounced, and challenged to duels.

Cable was born in New Orleans in 1844 to New England parents, and though his puritanical upbringing strongly inhibited his own behavior and outlook on life, he thoroughly understood and admired the gay, zestful Creoles. He also saw the blacks as human beings, with minds and talents often the equal of whites' (of whom many were blood relatives), and he was the first to dare to write of them in this way.

The Creoles could neither stand nor admit the truth of Cable's affectionate portrayal of them, and eventually drove him out of the city. After he moved to Massachusetts, his writing never again achieved

An 1872 mansion on Prytania Street is now occupied by the Louise McGehee School.

ABOVE: Bryan Bell house on Third Street, once the home of Michel Musson, uncle of Edgar Degas. LEFT: View from the lower gallery. OPPOSITE: The graceful floating staircase.

the quality that distinguished his southern work. The universal disdain for Cable's books among New Orleanians inspired one of them to begin a literary career of her own. Grace King began writing because of the challenge thrown down by a visiting magazine editor, who said, "If Cable is so false to you, why do not some of you write better?" Grace King was no more Creole than Cable, but her prolific outpouring

BELOW: Colonel Short's villa. LEFT: Gate in the villa's cornstalk fence.

Eighth Street raised cottage where George Washington Cable lived.

of prose, written from a Creole point of view, was immensely popular and respected. She is best known for *New Orleans: The Place and the People.* In her later years Grace King admitted that she had finally come to understand Cable, and that he "wrote too well about the Creoles."

The house in which Cable lived on Eighth Street has been restored by its owners as a private home. Although he was not esteemed in his own city, his worth was recognized by other writers, and Mark Twain, Joel Chandler Harris, and Lafcadio Hearn came to visit him there.

Michel Musson, uncle of the French Impressionist artist Edgar Degas, also lived in the Garden District. He purchased a site on Third Street in 1850 and reputedly commissioned James Gallier, Sr., to design the house, an Italianate villa interpreted in wood. Though he is known today only for his relationship to the renowned painter, Musson was an important man in New Orleans in his day. He was the city's postmaster, a prominent cotton merchant, and president of the Cotton Exchange. During a visit to New Orleans in 1872, Degas painted Musson's portrait as one of the group of men featured in a painting called "Cotton Factor's Office." It was during this visit that Degas's brother René married Estelle, one of Musson's four children. Their melodramatic tale is told in connection with Estelle's house on Esplanade Avenue (page 65).

The third owner, Charles M. Whitney, drastically altered the façade in 1884 by replacing the original copper-roofed bays with elaborate cast-ironwork. He also added a large Victorian building in the rear to stable his horses, named Comus and Momus, after two famous Carnival clubs, and Twenty-one, after a favorite riverboat game of chance.

One of the finest features of the house is the splendid, curving, free-hanging staircase. Below it is a tree decorated with Mardi Gras doubloons made by Mrs. Bryan Bell, wife of the current owner.

One of the finest and most famous mansions of the Garden District is the imposing house on the corner of Fourth and Prytania, renowned for its distinctive cornstalk fence. This magnificant example of cast-iron artistry encloses the extensive property in a design of cornstalks entwined with morning-glory vines and topped with large ears of corn. A duplicate casting of this exceptional fence adorns a French Quarter home that is now a guest house.

The house was built in 1859 for a wealthy commission merchant and Kentucky colonel, Robert Henry Short. It was designed by Henry Howard (architect of the Pontalba buildings and of the Farwell house on St. Charles Avenue) as an Italianate villa, adapted to its Deep South setting with the embellishment of handsome, elaborate iron-lace galleries. Its asymmetrical entrance opens onto an immense hallway, leading back to a graceful curving stairway. The architectural detail of its large-scale interiors is in the antebellum Greek Revival tradition. Though it has become known as "the cornstalk fence house," owner Thomas Favrot prefers to call it "Colonel Short's villa."

Though Garden District houses are highly valued, the elegant 1867 home of Mr. and Mrs. Sam Israel on First Street was in danger of demolition when Mrs. Sam Israel purchased it and undertook the extensive restoration required to revive its splendor. Missing pieces of ornate plasterwork that had been saved and stored in the attic were carefully replaced and restored by skilled local artisans. Also found in storage were the summer covers for the parlor fireplaces, with their petticoat mirrors—devised so that nineteenth-century ladies could check the hems of their floor-length gowns. Another important discovery was a decorative mural on the ceiling of the dining room, which had been hidden under wallpaper. A skull and crossbones under floorboards in the rear wing caused considerable excitement, but the Israels surmise that these were voodoo relics hidden by the servants rather than the remains of a murder victim.

It might be possible to find a nineteenth-century interior elsewhere in the country that resembles the Israels' beautiful parlor, but the façade, with its distinctive double columns joined by lacy cast-iron tracery, is unmistakably New Orleans.

54

Ballroom of the house on Prytania Street restored by Mr. and Mrs. Walter S. Simpson. It is now the home of Ella and Adelaide Brennan. The tile-framed fireplace shown opposite is in a room across the hall.

The interiors of Garden District homes were as richly decorated as the exteriors. Exceptional even among the great mansions of New Orleans is the splendid ballroom of the house at the corner of Second and Prytania streets that was restored by Mr. and Mrs. Walter S. Simpson. Almost a century after it was built in 1852, the house was ravaged by a fire that destroyed the tapestry decoration created for the ballroom ceiling by a Viennese artist. The Simpsons, who had just purchased the home, had the design carefully copied and restored in paint. Across the hall from the ballroom, the fire revealed another exceptional feature of the house that had been painted over—a unique set of tiles designed to frame the fireplace with scenes depicting Louisiana wildlife in its natural swamp setting.

Hidden behind the long, shuttered windows and fluted columns of a typical double-galleried Garden District façade is the serenely gracious parlor of the Pipes-Borah house on Philip Street. Twin white marble mantels are topped by massive gold-leaf framed mirrors that reflect the sparkle of matching crystal chandeliers hanging from the high ceilings on either side of the central arch. New Orleanians still call this lovely mid-nineteenth-century home the Pipes-Borah house because it once belonged to Federal Judge Wayne G. Borah, whose wife was a member of the Pipes family.

As the Garden District filled with elegant homes, building began to spread up St. Charles Avenue, and by the beginning of the twentieth century, the long, wide, double boulevard was lined with splendid houses from one end to the other. Unfortunately, so many of them have been destroyed (the city recently imposed a moratorium on demolition) that one can only admire those that remain and imagine how magnificent it was when the eighty or ninety blocks between Lee Circle and Carrollton Avenue comprised several miles of mansions. The property on which the handsome St. Charles Avenue house of Mr. and Mrs. F. Evans Farwell stands once belonged to Etienne de Boré, inventor of the sugar granulation process and first mayor after the Louisiana Purchase. And the house itself was owned by a descendant of Louisiana's first governor, William C. C. Claiborne. Set far back from the street, it is completely hidden by huge old magnolia trees. An excellent example of a late Greek Revival home in the indigenous raised-cottage style, it is little changed, and altogether typical of the graceful way of life in nineteenth-century New Orleans.

All the land along the river was originally occupied by several large plantations, but it was divided into lots and sold for suburban development. After Boré's death this property belonged to the New Orleans and Carrollton Railroad, which provided transportation up St. Charles Avenue (then called Nayades Street) from downtown. The railroad sold it to Antonio Palacio, who commissioned Henry Howard, architect of the Pontalba buildings, to design his residence in 1867. There have been very few structural changes since the house was completed in 1868. Originally the rear of the building was identical with the front:

58

OPPOSITE: Parlor of the Pipes-Borah house, now the home of Mr. and Mrs. Harry Merritt Lane, Jr.

ABOVE: Turn-of-the-century taste is exemplified in a St. Charles Avenue mansion built in 1896 and 1897. RIGHT: A detail of the porch.

Views of the F. Evans Farwell house. LEFT: The gallery.
ABOVE: Hallway. OPPOSITE: Exterior.

central stairs led down to a brick patio, where there was a kitchen building, servants' wing, a screened summer dining room, and cisterns. The kitchen was moved inside, and neither the rear stairway nor any of these outbuildings remain.

Mr. and Mrs. F. Evans Farwell, who bought the house in 1953, furnished it with family heirlooms that retain the authentic atmosphere of a New Orleans residence of this style and period. Mr. Farwell's

grandfather came from New England in the 1850s to establish the family shipping business, importing lime and ice from Maine to Louisiana. Many of the family antiques were brought to the city on the Farwell clipper ships.

The wide central hall of the Farwell house is typical of the antebellum plantation floor plan, providing much-needed cross ventilation in the hot South before air conditioning. As the coolest place in the house, it was often furnished and used as an auxiliary living room. The French Zuber wallpaper is from the 1920s Claiborne period of ownership, and the Oriental rugs have been in the Farwell family for several generations, as has the fine matching set of Belter furniture in the parlor. Henry Belter, a New York furniture maker between 1840 and 1860, invented a laminating process that made it possible to mold wood into the curved shapes that form the backs of his chairs. So strong was this laminated wood that the frames could be intricately carved and pierced and, reputedly, dropped from a second-story window onto a cobblestone street without breaking. Belter furniture was immensely popular in New Orleans, for besides being the height of fashion, it withstood the tropical heat and humidity. When other furniture makers began copying his work, Belter destroyed his molds and formula and retired, making genuine Belter furniture all the more rare and highly valued. Over the marble mantel in the parlor is a portrait of Mr. Farwell's great-grandfather, painted about 1840.

The imposing white Greek Revival mansion that is now the official residence of Tulane University presidents is among the few remaining of the many beautiful houses that formed an unbroken line up the oak-shaded boulevard of St. Charles Avenue. Though its circular drive sweeps up to the St. Charles Avenue door, it has an equally impressive entrance facing prestigious Audubon Place. Built by William T. Jay, whose English father had founded a highly successful Louisiana lumber company, the house was completed in the first years of the twentieth century. Since the Jays lived in the house for only ten years, it is not surprising that it is known by the name of its second owner, who bought it in 1917.

BELOW: Residence of the presidents of Tulane University. LEFT: Detail of the dining-room ceiling. BELOW, LEFT: Entrance hall.

Samuel Zemurray was the classic example of the rags-to-riches immigrant, and his acquisition of this beautiful home is a suitable happy ending to a success story. Born in Bessarabia in 1877, he came to the United States at the age of eleven and started working as assistant to a pack peddler, earning one dollar a week. He ultimately made a fortune in shipping bananas, becoming director of the United Fruit Company empire. He moved into this mansion at the age of forty and immediately began remodeling and embellishing the already grand house, paneling the library in walnut and adding the elaborate plaster ceilings. Though it is now difficult to imagine, the exterior of the house was originally dark brown brick and was not painted white until 1963.

Zemurray became a great philanthropist. One of his many generous gifts made possible the establishment of the important Middle American Research Institute of Tulane University, of which he was a long-time board member. When he died in 1961, he left this stately home on St. Charles Avenue to Tulane as a residence for the University presidents.

Bayou St. John and Esplanade Avenue

While the Garden District was being established by American society, Creoles began abandoning their Vieux Carré town houses to build their own Greek Revival mansions up Esplanade Avenue, the double boulevard that runs from the edge of the French Quarter out to Bayou St. John. As a result, the Vieux Carré went into a precipitous decline, and for several decades it was referred to scornfully as "French-town." The French Opera House burned in 1919, and the magnificent St. Louis Hotel fell into ruin. Bats and pigeons circled beneath the murals of its vast dome, and mules were stabled among the columns in the rotunda. Visiting writer John Galsworthy wrote a poem about encountering a white horse wandering through the interior of the once-grand hotel. Finally, in 1914, after a hurricane stripped the copper plating off the dome, causing plaster cornices to crumble and collapse, the St. Louis Hotel was demolished. The houses of the Vieux Carré fared little better, as poor black and immigrant Italian families kept chickens, goats, and even cows in the Pontalba buildings, and the fine dwellings of the city's first colonists became slums.

Esplanade Avenue was once as splendid as the American residential sector with which it competed. However, Esplanade suffered an even worse fate than St. Charles, and few of the fine Creole homes remain intact. An Esplanade Avenue house just beyond the French Quarter once belonged to Estelle Musson, daughter of Michel Musson (see page 54). After two decades in the Garden District the Mussons moved back downtown among their Creole friends.

Though blind from birth, Estelle had already been married and widowed when René and Edgar Degas arrived in New Orleans. René and Estelle fell in love, and a special dispensation had to be obtained from the Pope allowing the first cousins to marry. However, after the birth of their four children, René ran away with Estelle's best friend. Michel Musson adopted his four grandchildren, giving them his surname, and his daughter also resumed her maiden name. An unfinished portrait of Estelle Musson, painted by Edgar Degas, was recently purchased by the citizens of New Orleans and now hangs in the Delgado Museum, in City Park, at the end of Esplanade Avenue.

Estelle's elegant house, which boasts nine marble mantels and some of the city's largest ceiling medallions, had been turned into a tenement with seven apartments, and suffered hurricane damage just prior to its restoration in 1967 by its present owner, C. J. Blanda.

At the end of Esplanade Avenue, along the banks of Bayou St. John, near City Park (which was once the Allard plantation), are some of the earliest homes remaining in the city. The dates of these buildings are vague, because city records go back only to about 1822, and although it is sometimes possible to trace ownership of property, it is difficult to be sure when structures were built on the land, and whether they are the existing buildings or earlier ones. However, at least three of those still standing were built prior to 1800. The so-called Spanish Custom House at 1300 Moss Street is generally considered the

Houses on Esplanade Avenue.

In the home of Mr. C. J. Blanda, the past elegance of Esplanade Avenue
has been restored.

earliest; some say it may have been erected about 1784, while others estimate a date between the 1750s
and 1780s. It was built as a small plantation house in the French West Indies style, by Don Santiago
Lloreins, and no one knows why it was called a custom house, because there is no record that it ever was one.

At 924 Moss Street is a house that once was part of an extensive plantation with one hundred
and fifty slaves. Though a structure is indicated on this land as far back as 1767, the present building was
not constructed until the late 1790s, after Louis Blanc bought the property from Don Almonaster y
Roxas. The house is built on brick pyramids, with walls three bricks thick. Outer walls on the ground
floor are stucco over brick, while the upstairs walls are *briqueté entre poteaux,* also covered with stucco.
The house has a one-story colonnaded *garçonnière* and a separate outbuilding across the back of its enclosed
garden. The stairway is a 1930 addition, but the present owners have taken most of the house back to its
earliest period, uncovering old mantels and brick and tile flooring.

A son of Louis Blanc built the larger, grander home at 1342 Moss Street. A Greek Revival modi-
fication of the earlier Bayou plantation style, it was donated to the Catholic Church in 1905 by Blanc's
descendants. Two other early plantation houses along the Bayou also became church property; one was
demolished to make way for a modern Catholic school, and the other, Pitot House, was rescued and
moved to a new site by the Louisiana Landmarks Society.

Built just prior to 1800, the Pitot house at 1440 Moss Street is a typical West Indies plantation
home. James Pitot, who bought it in 1810, was the second owner of the house. He came to New Orleans
in 1796 as a refugee from a slave uprising in Santo Domingo that brought a large influx of émigrés to

Louisiana. New Orleans' first elected mayor after the Louisiana Purchase, Pitot was later appointed to a judgeship by Governor Claiborne.

Pitot bought the plantation house, with thirty acres of land, as a country home for his family. The building conforms to the indigenous Louisiana raised-cottage style, with the major rooms for living elevated well above the ground. Its walls are brick-between-posts, covered with stucco. Deep galleries shade the front and sides, colonnaded with round, stuccoed columns below, and lighter wood colonnettes above. There is an enclosed loggia across the rear, with a jalousie-screened gallery. The rooms, which run the full depth of the house, have French doors opening onto the wide porches.

In 1962 the building, which had been used as a nuns' residence by the Missionary Sisters of the Sacred Heart, was threatened with demolition. The house was offered to the Louisiana Landmarks Society, with the provision that it be moved from the site where construction of a new school was planned. With the cooperation of the city, the Society obtained the corner of an adjacent playground, and the house was moved on a flatbed truck. The columns were transported intact, with corsets of two-by-fours strapped around them for support. The bottom of the house had to be reconstructed (in exact replica) to receive the original top. Restoration took ten years, during which Hurricane Betsy tore off the roof, and vandals broke windows and damaged the house. It was decided that a live-in curator was needed, and so the Society persuaded James D. Didier to move from a house he had restored in the Vieux Carré (page 129) to

Holy Rosary Rectory, 1342 Moss Street, built c. 1834, is one of the early houses
remaining on Bayou St. John.

The Louis Blanc house, 924 Moss Street, from the rear. BELOW: The ground-floor living room. OPPOSITE: The hall and stairway.

Pitot House. RIGHT: The dining room. OPPOSITE: The front façade and (below) the entrance hall. Above the desk is a portrait of James Pitot.

live in the Pitot house with his wife and children. It was a fortuitous arrangement in more ways than one, because the Society had acquired only a few pieces with which to furnish the house, and the Didiers owned a museum-quality collection of early Louisiana furniture. Didier designed all the interiors, and his wife made the lovely swags, draperies, and bed hangings. The fact that a family lives in the beautifully furnished period restoration gives it a quality that no museum can hope to duplicate. Pitot House is open to the public one day a week or at other times by appointment.

On the wall by the front door hangs a portrait of James Pitot. The slant-top desk, an ancestral piece from Mrs. Didier's family, is "Louisiana made," of magnolia wood. Over the fireplace is a picture of George Washington, reverse-painted on glass.

An original Audubon print of the yellow-crowned heron hangs in the dining room. The dining table is identical with one owned by Andrew Jackson, and the chairs are in the style of François Seignouret. Over the table hangs a cypress punkah, a device designed to be moved back and forth during meals to keep flies away, operated by a servant pulling its rope. The dining-room china is Old Paris, an early Louisiana favorite.

Ghosts and Legends

While the cream of Creole society was performing its rituals of dining, entertaining, and mating, there was another well-established social custom flourishing in the famous Quadroon Balls. Existing in New Orleans was a large, respected element of society (at its peak it numbered 1700 in a total population of 5000) known as *gens de couleur,* or free people of color. These people took pride in their status, writing the initials f.m.c. or f.w.c. (free man of color or free woman of color) after their names, and were so described in birth records. Most were more white than black in their parentage: not only a half, but three-quarters or seven-eighths, called quadroon or octaroon. Some of the more affluent *gens de couleur* owned large plantations, along with the slaves needed to work the land.

Beautiful young quadroon girls were raised by their mothers, much as courtesans were in France, to become the mistresses of white gentlemen. The courting procedure took place at the Quadroon Balls, where Creole gentlemen came to dance and woo the girls of their choice. Upon choosing, arrangements were made through the girls' mothers and were considered as binding as marriage agreements. Included was setting up the young lady in a house of her own and providing for her future, as well as for any children she might bear. The gentleman visited his mistress in her *petite maison* (many of these houses still stand today in the Faubourg Marigny) until he married, and sometimes even afterward, for marriages, always arranged as social and financial alliances, were often unhappy, while relationships with quadroon mistresses were based on love and/or sexual attraction. However, when mistresses were forsaken by their white lovers, they were free to marry men of color while continuing to live in the homes provided by their lovers. These quadroon mistresses flaunted their exceptional beauty, riding about the town in carriages, elegantly dressed, and wearing particularly elaborate headdresses. Creole women became so incensed at this feminine competition that they demanded a law prohibiting women of color from wearing anything but a kerchief (known as a *tignon*) on their heads. However, quadroons circumvented this ruling by affecting ever more colorful and extravagant *tignons*.

Marie Laveau, daughter of the quadroon mistress of a white man, became the most powerful and famous queen of the voodoo cult in North America—because New Orleans was certainly the only city on this continent where the black arts imported from Africa and the Indies became so widely practiced and so deeply entrenched. Her tomb, in the St. Louis Cemetery No. 1, marked with the name of her second husband, Glapion, is always covered with brick-dust X-marks that are supposed to bring good luck. Whenever these marks are wiped off, they immediately reappear. Voodoo was based on black magic, charms (or *gris-gris*), and good and evil spirits embodied in the symbol of a snake. Though its practitioners and chief adherents were blacks, whites sometimes sought its help in times of desperation, such as unrequited love affairs, or during the frightful yellow-fever epidemics. Voodoo dances were held weekly in Congo Square on the city outskirts just above Rampart Street, until they were banned. However, there is no question that voodoo continued and perhaps still thrives today. In the mid-1930s writer Lyle Saxon wangled a catalogue of charms for sale from a voodoo drugstore and published a list of seventy-five items available at prices ranging from 25¢ to $2.50, including love powder, war powder, anger powder, peace powder, gambler's luck, luck around business, dragon's blood, and goofer dust (earth from a grave).

Marie Laveau's tomb in St. Louis Cemetery No. 1.

The Haunted House at 1140 Royal Street.

OPPOSITE: Oven vaults in St. Louis Cemetery No. 1.
BELOW: Their counterparts in Lafayette Cemetery.

Small wonder that blacks looked for supernatural help in a society where they were at the mercy of the whites who owned them, even though strict codes had existed from the time of Bienville's administration regulating the care and keeping of slaves. Most slave owners took good care of their valuable property, treating slaves in a paternalistic manner, but slaves could all too easily fall helpless victims to any psychological aberration of their masters.

The oft-told tale of the Haunted House at 1140 Royal Street is the most extreme example. This was the home of Madame Lalaurie, a legendary Creole beauty of the finest social background, renowned as a hostess, cultured and charming. She entertained Lafayette, among others, in her sumptuously decorated home. In view of her status, scant attention was paid to rumors of strange screams and cries in the night that emanated from her imposing mansion, in spite of the fact that a female black child fell from the rooftop to her death in the courtyard below after neighbors claimed they heard her footsteps running through the house as she was pursued by someone cracking a whip.

The horrible truth was revealed in 1834 when a fire broke out in Madame Lalaurie's house. A crowd gathered as neighbors helped carry out precious furnishings, paintings, and *objets d'art* under Madame Lalaurie's direction. In spite of the lady's objections, neighbors insisted on searching for servants who

The former Louisiana Jockey Club, built in 1865 as the Luling Mansion.

LEFT: Metairie Cemetery.

might be trapped in the burning house. They found a torture chamber in the attic, where mutilated slaves were chained in positions that permanently deformed their twisted bodies. The cook, found chained in the kitchen, had started the fire, preferring to burn to death rather than to continue living under the lash of her sadistic mistress. Apparently, the charming, exquisite Madame Lalaurie was known to have excused herself from balls or dinner parties to go upstairs and gratify her lust for torture. (A later explanation offered for this cruel perversion was that her mother, who started the first school for blacks, had been murdered in a black uprising.)

The crowd outside the house, expecting the police, who never arrived, was surprised by a carriage that burst forth from the driveway and raced down the street with Madame Lalaurie inside. She was never seen in New Orleans again. The angry crowd vented its rage and frustration upon the house, smashing the handsome interiors. Afterward the house was used as Union headquarters during the Civil War; it then became a gambling casino in the 1870s. Next it served as a home for the destitute, before its recent conversion to apartments. Throughout the years it reputedly has been haunted by Madame Lalaurie's miserable victims. There has been a variety of stories recounting strange lights, and shadowy objects with skeleton heads, while hoarse voices and clanking chains were heard emanating from the servants' quarters.

The prejudices that kept Creoles and Americans apart in life separated them even in death, for both had their own cemeteries. Early settlers had begun burying their dead just behind the cathedral, but as increasing demand for space made this impractical, the first cemetery, St. Louis No. 1, was established just outside the city walls (on the other side of Rampart Street). Eventually overcrowding with yellow-fever and dueling victims necessitated the addition of an adjacent cemetery, St. Louis No. 2, and later St. Louis No. 3. When the Protestant Americans arrived, they began burying their dead in Lafayette Cemetery in the Garden District.

Though the oldest are the most fascinating and picturesque, the unique early cemeteries of New Orleans have much in common. Underground burial prior to the invention of modern perpetual drainage systems was difficult, if not impossible. Coffins almost floated before they could be buried; a grisly quotation from an early letter tells of boring holes in a coffin and having large blacks stand on it until it sank and settled into the swampy ground. So it became customary for all burial to be above ground in tombs. This created a problem for the less wealthy that was solved in several ways. Families had double vaults, one above the other. Several years after burial in the top vault, the bones could be removed to the lower vault while the upper one was reused. Various societies or organizations banded together to build large compartmented tombs for members. And finally, the poor could rent space in the "oven" vaults that form the outer walls surrounding the cemeteries like apartment houses in these cities of the dead. Some think they were called oven vaults because of their shape, but another theory is that the hot tropical sun baked the remains in these brick enclosures.

Like the homes of the living, all tombs were built of brick, plastered over and whitewashed. Since stone had to be imported, it was used only for ornamental sculpture, with thin marble slabs for the French inscriptions. Wrought iron was also used to adorn tombs, with gates and crosses providing stark contrast against the white monuments. In the early Creole cemeteries tombs were erected haphazardly, crowded along winding, zigzagging paths, without plan or order. Once a year, on All Saints' Day, a holiday taken seriously in New Orleans as it is in France, Creole Catholics bring flowers, pull weeds from crevices, and whitewash the tombs.

There are many similar cemeteries near the end of Canal Street. Metairie, one of the largest, grandest, and most recent American cemeteries, was once a racetrack. It was converted to a cemetery as an act of revenge, when a wealthy man named Howard, ironically spurned because his money came from running the lottery, was refused membership in the exclusive Jockey Club (which still stands, as a somewhat shabby apartment house, just off the upper end of Esplanade Avenue). Metairie Cemetery is also the site of the tomb of famous madam Josie Arlington. Citizens were tantalized when a red light appeared on her opulent monument after it was completed, but this supposed supernatural phenomenon turned out to be just the reflection of a traffic light across the street.

Tombs in St. Louis Cemetery No. 1.

Josie Arlington was only one of the many flamboyant madams who presided over the lavishly decorated houses of ill repute that flourished at the turn of the century in New Orleans' heyday as the capital of sin. An impressive statistic reveals that there were 190,000 brothels in the city at this time; scarcely a block was without at least one. To prevent bordellos from proliferating in respectable neighborhoods, an ordinance was passed, introduced by Alderman Sidney Story, confining such establishments to a limited area in the vicinity of Basin Street (which, along with Rampart, had been an elegant residential area prior to its invasion by ladies of the night). To the alderman's chagrin, the nation's most notorious red-light district was nicknamed Storyville. The name stuck, and Alderman Story was immortalized forever.

This experiment in controlled, legal prostitution produced *The Blue Book*, which, like the Yellow Pages, listed and advertised all the houses with copious adjectives and illustrations, describing their various attractions, and star performers. The establishments were housed in fashionable brownstones, opulently decorated with plush, gilt, and marble, and furnished with Oriental rugs and grand pianos. The city's most important men were entertained, in evening dress, and no visitor would consider leaving town without seeing the famous houses of Storyville. All of them have since been demolished; Basin Street, formerly the center of what was Storyville, is now only a wide, somewhat characterless boulevard one block above Rampart Street.

OPPOSITE AND ABOVE: Double and single shotgun cottages and a typical cottage porch bracket.

During World War I the U.S. Navy Department forced the city to close down the notorious district, and so the days of the illustrious madams came to an end. However, by that time "Countess" Willie Piazza had already complained that "the country club girls are ruining my business." The houses were once more scattered throughout the city. Returned to an illegal basis, prostitutes went back to paying off police and city officials, some of whom actually sponsored the girls through lean periods. At some of the more modest cribs in the Quarter, piles of bills and change could be seen left out on the doorsteps for collection in the early morning.

Storyville was the birthplace of jazz. The best brothels employed bands of from two to four players to entertain their customers, while others made do with wandering groups of itinerant musicians. Among the itinerants was a group of seven teenagers who called themselves the Spasm Band. They used crude, makeshift instruments; a piece of lead pipe doubled as a megaphone, a fiddle was made of a cigar box, the bass was a contraption constructed from half a barrel, and the percussion consisted of an old kettle, a cowbell, and a gourd full of pebbles. The muscians' colorful names included Stalebread Charley, Warm Gravy, Whiskey, Cajun, Monk, and Chinee. When "Jazzy" was added to their slogan, "The Razzy Dazzy Spasm Band," the name stuck and has since identified the music created in the brothels of New Orleans at the turn of the century. New Orleans–born Louis Armstrong, as he traveled the world with his hot trumpet and gravelly voice, elevated jazz to an internationally appreciated art form.

While the madams entertained in their mansions and society retired to what were then the suburbs, less affluent citizens went home to the more humble dwellings known as shotgun cottages. Peculiar

83

RIGHT: Doorway of Captain Thomas P. Leathers' house on Carondolet Street. OPPOSITE: The present-day *Natchez*.

BELOW: Fanciful "steamboat" house on Egania Street, one of a pair built by Captain M. Paul Doullut for himself and his son.

to New Orleans, these simple structures were built all over the city during the nineteenth century. The name derives from the floor plan: one room lines up behind another in a row, so that a shot fired through the front door would exit through the rear without hitting anything en route. Variations on the style include the basic single shotgun, the double (two singles joined to make a two-family house), and the camelback, which is either a single or a double but has a second story added to the rear section of the house. Façade decorations vary from simple, plain porch columns to elaborate gingerbread brackets supporting the porch roof. In recent years these cottages have become immensely popular, particularly among young people, who convert them into extremely attractive homes, often by removing interior partitions to open up the space. Though many are strikingly contemporary, others have been beautifully decorated in period styles and furnished with antiques, such as the home of interior designer Rivet Hedderel, shown in color on page 98.

New Orleans was probably as famous for its outlaws, underworld, and crime in general as any of the world's most notorious seaports, vying with Shanghai and Marseilles for that dubious honor. There is the tragic tale of a handsome young society gentleman who ventured into fearful Gallatin Street for a lark on the eve of his wedding and was never seen again. Years later it was learned that he was shanghaied—an all too common occurrence, along with robbery, murder, and mayhem. As far back as the mid-nineteenth century, serious consideration was given to discontinuing Mardi Gras because crime was so uncontrollable. The city's most legendary outlaw was, of course, Jean Lafitte, the pirate. Originally Lafitte's activities were quite legitimate; he was a privateer, with French letters of marque that gave him a legal right to plunder enemy ships. However, he inevitably branched out to attack friendly vessels, and he also

85

began an extensive, highly profitable business in smuggling his looted merchandise. The charming little Creole cottage in Bourbon Street known as Lafitte's Blacksmith Shop was allegedly a cover for his illegal activities in the city, though his main base of operations was at Barataria in the Delta. There are so many myths surrounding Lafitte's name that it is impossible to distinguish fact from fiction. Apparently he and his men did join in helping to defeat the British at the Battle of New Orleans in 1815—although this famous battle in fact proved to be a total waste of time and lives, as it was fought before word arrived that a treaty had already been signed. The tomb of Lafitte's chief lieutenant, Dominique You, who reformed and became respectable, may be seen in St. Louis Cemetery No. 2.

Two inventions of the late eighteenth century had a major effect on New Orleans' economy. Discovery in 1795 by Etienne de Boré of a means to granulate sugar from the juice of sugar cane added new fortunes to those already being made from cotton, thanks to Eli Whitney's invention of the cotton gin. But unparalleled prosperity really arrived in New Orleans with the first steamboat in 1812. By 1820 there were 60 steamboats; in 1834 their number had increased to 230, and in another ten years there were 450. The wharves were lined with rows of them, two or three deep as they waited to load cargo which could now be transported *up* the river as well as down.

At first no one imagined that these so-called "swimming volcanoes" would ever carry passengers. But before long, steamboats were vying with each other in the elegance of their accommodations and food. The menus were staggering, and the steamboats began to be known as floating palaces instead of "swimming volcanoes." Colorful riverboat gamblers made fortunes by voyaging up and down, swindling wealthy passengers out of huge sums of money. Steamboat races became the passion of the era, as proud captains competed fiercely, and people lined the levees and riverbanks for miles to watch them go by. Some dreadful tragedies occurred during these races, when overheated boilers exploded, scalding and killing numerous passengers.

The race to end all races took place in 1870, when the *Robert E. Lee* beat the *Natchez* to St. Louis. Captain John Cannon had stripped all the upper works of the *Robert E. Lee,* refused passengers and freight, and arranged to be met along the way by flatboats bearing fuel. The handsome home of the loser, Captain Leathers, can still be seen on Carondelet Street, in the block behind the Pontchartrain Hotel, and, of course, the race will always be remembered by the song, "waitin' on the levee, waitin' for the Robert E. Lee."

The steamboat era, the pinnacle of New Orleans' prosperity, began to wane when the Erie Canal provided means of shipping goods from the Great Lakes to eastern ports. But it was the competition of the railroads that put an end to the opulent floating palaces, just as the airlines later ruined the trade of railroads and ocean liners. The vast wealth that poured into the port city at the mouth of the Mississippi began to spread to other cities.

The city had continued to thrive (1830 to 1860 was considered its golden age) despite the yellow-fever plagues that killed enormous numbers of the population throughout the nineteenth century. These days of unimaginable horror are best described through the words of a heroic minister, Theodore Clapp, who managed to escape the dread disease even though he worked day after day around the clock to help its victims:

> I found at the graveyard a large pile of corpses without coffins, in horizontal layers, one above the other, like corded wood. I was told that there were more than one hundred bodies deposited there. . . . Large trenches were dug, into which these uncoffined corpses were thrown indiscriminately. . . . A private hospital was found deserted; the physicians, nurses and attendants were all dead, or had run away. Not a living person was in it. The wards were filled with putrid bodies, which, by order of the Mayor, were piled in an adjacent yard, and burned, and their ashes scattered to the winds. . . .
>
> I went one Wednesday night, to solemnize the contract of marriage between a couple of very genteel appearance. The bride was young and possessed of the most extraor-

Cast-iron cistern reconstructed behind the
Hermann-Grima house in the French Quarter.

An old plantation cistern replaces
the original at Gallier House.

Cargo ship at the levee near Audubon Park.

dinary beauty. A few hours only had elapsed before I was summoned to perform the last offices over her coffin. . . . One family, of nine persons, supped together in perfect health; at the expiration of the next twenty-four hours, eight of the nine were dead. . . . Persons were found dead all along the streets, particularly early in the mornings. . . .

Nature seemed to sympathize in the dreadful spectacle of human woe. A thick, dark atmosphere . . . hung over us like a mighty funereal shroud. . . . The burning of tar and pitch at every corner; the firing of cannon, by order of the city authorities, along all the streets; and the frequent conflagrations which actually occurred at that dreadful period—all these conspired to add a sublimity and horror to the tremendous scene.

These incredibly horrible epidemics hit the city thirty-nine times between 1796 and 1906, lasting for weeks or even months at a time, until finally it was discovered that mosquitoes, breeding copiously in the open cisterns and ditches, were the carriers of yellow fever. The cisterns that stood behind houses to collect rainwater were destroyed, and oil was poured in ditches and on other still or stagnant water to kill the mosquitoes.

The final blow to New Orleans, however, was neither plague nor railroads but the Civil War. The entire economy of the South had been based on slaves working the vast lands of cotton and sugar plantations. So along with the death of its young manhood, the pillage and destruction of war, and the cruel revenge of the Reconstruction era, the very foundations of southern prosperity were overturned. Where there were once more than a hundred plantation houses along the river in the ninety miles between New Orleans and Baton Rouge, only a dozen or so remain. A way of life was ended, and recovery took many years. Symbolizing the change is the crumbling ruin of lovely Sevenoaks Plantation, ringed with giant oil tanks, and the huge, ugly, smoky industrial plants surrounding the remains of another once-lordly plantation below the city. Less cruel and inhuman than a feudal economy based on slavery, to be sure, but certainly also less picturesque and beautiful to look upon.

Feasts and Festivals

In recent decades a new source of wealth has come to New Orleans. Tourists, attracted by the charming atmosphere of the French Quarter, the superb cuisine of fine restaurants, and the excitement of Mardi Gras, spend freely in the city.

A large part of Creole social life always centered in food, and its importance in New Orleans has never been even remotely approached anywhere else in America. Creole cuisine was developed in the city's early days, and though it seems elaborate, extravagant, and excessively rich to visitors used to plain American fare, it pales in comparison with the overwhelming meals served in the eighteenth and nineteenth centuries.

The only American cooking tradition worthy of being called a cuisine was born of three major factors: the unparalleled plenty of native ingredients, particularly seafood; the mixture of nationalities that made up the city; and the strong influence of the French, who take eating very seriously indeed. In 1727 the same Ursuline nun who described the appearance of the crude frontier settlement listed the food available in the colony: ". . . wild beef, venison, swans, geese, fowls, ducks, sarcelles [a type of small wild duck], pheasants, partridges, *cailles* [small birds similar to partridges], and fish: cat, carp, bass, salmon, besides infinite varieties not known in France." There were "wild peas and beans and rice; pineapples, watermelons, potatoes, *sabotins* (a kind of eggplant), figs, bananas, pecans, pumpkins." They drank "chocolate and café au lait every day," and ate "bread made of rice or corn mixed with flour . . . and sagamité [an early form of jambalaya]."

Add to this impressive list the shrimp, oysters, crabs, red fish, trout, okra, mirlitons—begin with basic French cuisine, stir in pinches of Spanish and Italian, some strong flavoring of African and of American Indian, and you have the incomparable, inimitable cuisine called Creole.

One of the dishes for which New Orleans is so justly famous is gumbo, served in a soup bowl with a teacup-molded mound of rice in the center and surrounded by crab claws full of succulent meat. Gumbo, originally "gombo," illustrates the combination of multinational influences and native ingredients involved in the development of Creole cuisine. This New Orleans variation on bouillabaisse replaces with Gulf crabs, shrimp, and oysters the assortment of Mediterranean fish used in the French soup. Addition of either okra or filé gives the gumbo soup stock its distinctive texture. Filé, made from powdered sassafras leaves, is an ingredient borrowed from the Choctaw Indians, and other spicy flavorings undoubtedly came from Spanish, West Indian, and African cuisines. Though gumbo is called a soup, it is a meal in itself. Red Fish Courtbouillon is a popular Louisiana dish created to exploit the qualities of this delicious large fish, so abundant in native waters. *Café brûlot* represents another New Orleans tradition and is so special that it has its own chafing dish and ladle, and cups designed specifically for serving it.

New Orleans coffee has a mystique all its own. Dripped very slowly and often blended with chicory, it is preferred "so strong that the spoon will stand up in it," or "black as the devil and hot as hell." This latter expression and the alternate name, *café brûlot diabolique,* explains why the devil motif decorates *brûlot* cups, and devil figurines form the footed base of the *brûlot* chafing dish. *Café brûlot* is made from very strong coffee added to a flaming mixture of brandy, sugar, cinnamon, cloves, and citrus peel (or, in some cases, a decorative ribbon of orange peel studded with cloves).

New Orleans' (and perhaps America's) oldest and most famous restaurant is Antoine's. Founded in 1840 by Antoine Alciatore, it has always been run by members of the same family, in the same old building with ironwork balconies on St. Louis Street in the French Quarter. Like Commander's Palace in the Garden District, the restaurant began as a dining room for guests housed upstairs, but the food superseded the lodgers, who are now long gone and forgotten.

Young Antoine emigrated from France, where he had served an apprenticeship in hotel kitchens, bringing with him many recipes, including that for his marvelously inflated potatoes called *pommes soufflées.* He also invented others to add to a menu that is still printed entirely in French. Pompano *en papillote,* with the fish covered with a sauce of shrimp and wine and baked in a sealed parchment envelope, one of the dishes served to President Franklin D. Roosevelt at Antoine's, was the joint conception of Antoine and his son, Jules. Jules's most celebrated creation was the much imitated but unequaled Oysters Rockefeller, which he devised as an American replacement for *escargots à la bourguignonne.*

Though most tourists know only Antoine's large, French-style, tile-floored front room, with its ceiling fans and brass chandeliers, the restaurant rambles on through room after room, filled with hundreds of photographs of famous guests who have dined there during nearly a century and a half.

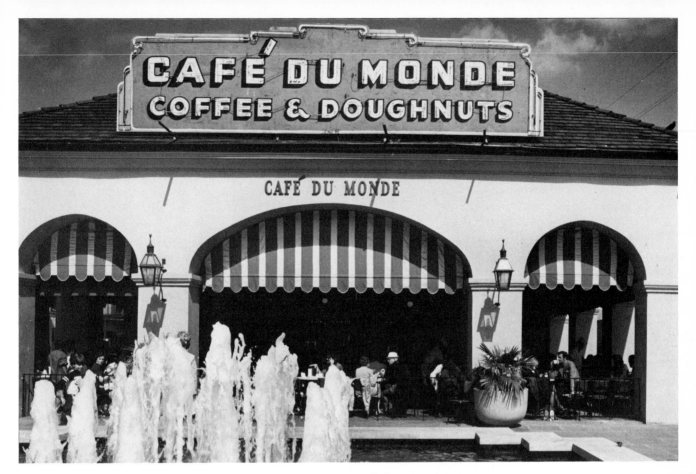

OPPOSITE AND ABOVE: "Doughnuts," in New Orleans, means *beignets,* crisp fritters which can turn a coffee break into an occasion.

The history of the building at 417 Royal Street that now houses Brennan's Restaurant is an intriguing one, liberally laced with misfortune. Built as a residence in 1801 by Don José Faurie, it was sold to the Bank of Louisiana in 1805. The bank's initials may still be seen in the ironwork. Fifteen years later it became the home of Martin Gordon, who entertained Andrew Jackson there in 1828. When Gordon suffered financial reverses, the building became the home of Judge Alonzo Morphy, whose famous son Paul was recognized as a chess genius by the time he was ten years old. He became the world's greatest chess player, but died at the age of forty-seven, broken in mind and health. The next owner, W. Ratcliffe Irby, shot himself in a mortuary after selecting and purchasing his own casket.

The so-called Morphy house, willed to Tulane University by Irby, was then leased for a number of years to a restaurant called Patio Royal; until it was taken over by Owen Brennan in 1955. Brennan dreamed of expanding the spectacularly successful French restaurant he had started in small quarters on Bourbon Street into a truly elegant establishment. With the help of the architectural firm of Koch and Wilson, and interior designer Charles Gresham, he undertook a restoration that transformed the old house into the most beautiful restaurant in New Orleans. But the evil curse struck again, and Owen died of a sudden heart attack on the eve of its opening. The Brennan family carried on, establishing a tremendously popular restaurant, and it seemed that at last the malevolent spirits had been exorcised . . . until a fire severely damaged the building, closing Brennan's down for half the year in 1975.

Aside from its exceptionally good, traditional Creole food, the charm of Dunbar's, on St. Charles Avenue, is that eating there is like being invited into a private home. Originally Corinne Dunbar, a Creole

Antoine's.

Royal Street. In the center is Brennan's Restaurant.

lady whose means were pinched by hard times, began serving meals in her own home, on family china and silverware. The excellent fare and pleasant setting were so much appreciated by New Orleanians that Corinne Dunbar's formally became a restaurant and was carried on after her death by a relative, James Plauché. Its lunches and dinners are by reservation only. There is no signboard on the double-galleried Greek Revival house, and guests must ring the doorbell to be ushered into a Victorian parlor where they may order drinks before being shown to their tables. This double parlor, with its high ceiling and elaborate plaster decoration on the dividing arch and ceiling medallions, is typical of interiors built in the latter part of the nineteenth century in New Orleans and other American cities. The meal is served in a handsome dining room decorated with carved marble mantels and Baccarat crystal Empire chandeliers, and neither a menu nor a bill is presented at the table.

At Commander's Palace restaurant in the heart of the Garden District, musicians stroll among the tables, entertaining weekend diners with soft, muted jazz. This delightful custom was inaugurated by Ella, Adelaide, Dick, and John Brennan, after they took over the large, rambling old restaurant from the former owner, Mrs. Frank Moran. Commander's history of fine dining goes back to 1880, when Emile Commander began serving meals in the large Victorian building where he ran a lodging house. The restaurant passed through one other ownership, and then, in 1944, the Morans began developing it into an award-winning dining establishment of wide renown. Mrs. Moran left some distinctive decorating touches, such as the crystal and Victorian chandeliers, and the bronze herons in the patio pool, but her most unusual contribution was the addition of the enormous garden with its giant trees and tropical foliage. Members of the Brennan clan, who launched the successful French Quarter restaurant, are now working their magic on this venerable institution opposite Lafayette Cemetery with equally positive results.

Apart from the restaurants, probably the most magnetic attraction in New Orleans is Mardi Gras. Like the Vieux Carré, Mardi Gras was not devised for the benefit or entertainment of tourists. Though it may be hard to believe, the extravagant, costly display that begins to unfold with Twelfth Night in early January and culminates in the Tuesday that falls forty days before Easter is prepared solely for the amusement of its participants. And yet "amusement" is scarcely the appropriate word, for it is taken very seriously, as indeed it must be, for it requires a full year and huge sums of money, without any commercial sponsorship whatever. The extravagant parades and balls of Mardi Gras are the productions of exclusive men's clubs called krewes, their leadership made up of the cream of society. This society is the outgrowth of intermarriages between Creoles and Anglo-Saxons which took place as the European descendants of early colonists at last bowed to the necessity of mingling their proud blood with that of the prosperous, industrious Americans. However, just as the powerful French cultural influence survived Spanish domination, the Creole strain has had an obvious, lasting effect on the Anglo-Saxon. The French language has all but vanished, except for the Cajun patois of the Delta country spoken by the descendants of exiles driven out of the French Acadian settlements of eastern Canada in the eighteenth century. But the prevailing spirit behind Mardi Gras, like the custom itself, is completely Latin—and the easy-going, party-loving character of New Orleanians is unquestionably inherited from the Creoles.

Though celebration of the occasion has been going on in New Orleans since 1766, parading on Mardi Gras day was introduced to New Orleans in 1857 by six men from Mobile, Alabama, who belonged to a society that had been parading there since 1831. The first and still the most socially prestigious krewe that was formed was Comus. Men who belong to these Carnival organizations choose a King and court each year from the most socially prominent members in their club, and their names are a closely guarded secret that keeps society guessing and gossiping until Carnival day. The Queen and her court, daughters of members, are chosen from the season's debutantes. The lavish costumes, robes, and regalia, made to order and

paid for by the participants, are understandably costly, and many a socially prominent family in reduced circumstances has had to defer the grocer's bill to finance them. Past as well as present Kings and Queens are allowed to fly the purple, green, and gold carnival flag from their homes on Mardi Gras day, and often display the royal trappings of their moment of glory in glass cases or even on dress forms in a place of honor in their homes.

There are many organizations that give balls, beginning in early January, and all parades terminate in balls, involving elaborate tableaux and dancing among krewe members and society ladies whom they "call out." The ladies' escorts and other invited guests may only sit in the balcony and watch. Admission to the balls, by invitation only, is exclusive, particularly to the prestigious Comus; the court of Comus ritually meets with the court of Rex at midnight on Mardi Gras night, at the conclusion of the year's festivities. The maskers on horseback and those on the floats in costumes are all members of the organization giving the parade. The maskers throw beads, trinkets, and Mardi Gras "doubloons" (coins specially made to commemorate each parade) to the spectators. Members of both Rex and Comus are also members of the exclusive Boston Club; no man can reign as King of Carnival without being a member of the Boston Club. The club has kept the male supreme in the city's social fabric. Rex's Queen and her court traditionally sit in a balcony erected on the front of the club on Mardi Gras day, and the King's float pauses there while he toasts his Queen with champagne.

Only wars have ever prevented the tradition of Mardi Gras; it was suspended for a few years during the Civil War and during World War II. However, in 1885, beset by financial difficulties due to Reconstruction, Comus was forced to suspend its parade and ball, and Momus took over Comus's precedented Mardi Gras evening parade time. The following year, when Momus also went under, Proteus moved up from Monday to Tuesday night, enjoying the ritual meeting with the Court of Rex, and consequently becoming the most socially important organization.

Comus returned in 1890 and demanded that Proteus put its ball and parade back to Monday, allowing Comus to resume its rightful place on Tuesday, crowning the peak of Carnival festivities. Proteus refused, provoking a deadly serious yet somehow hilarious confrontation. Since members of Proteus had already engaged the French Opera House for their ball, Comus arranged to hold theirs in the Grand Opera House, but the parades presented a more difficult problem. Each krewe tried to outdo the other, and a race to reach Canal Street ensued. Proteus, arriving first, paraded down one side of Canal Street, while Comus paraded up the other, creating a spectacle of double magnitude, as glittering floats lined both sides of the wide boulevard, with bands playing different music simultaneously.

At the corner of Canal and Bourbon, where the parades turned to enter the French Quarter on the way to their respective ballrooms, there was a confrontation. The floats met, and neither would give way. While the Kings glared at each other over their beards, the krewe captains (who really run the show) rode up on their horses and engaged in a violent argument. A fight between the maskers threatened to break out, and the crowds began laughing. The impasse was solved by allowing the parades to proceed by alternating floats. Rex, faced with the problem of whose court to meet at the midnight climax of the balls, resolved the dilemma by going to both, but chose to attend Comus first. For one more year both krewes held their parades and balls the same night, but after that, Proteus yielded Tuesday night back to Comus, allowing the traditional rituals of more than a century of Mardi Gras celebrations to return to their strange and wonderful routine.

Sala Capitular of the Cabildo

BELOW: Renovated interior of a nineteenth-century shotgun cottage. RIGHT: Parlor of the F. Evans Farwell house. RIGHT, BELOW: Dining room and parlor of the Hermann-Grima house. OPPOSITE PAGE: Double parlor of the Israel house.

RIGHT: Royal Street. BELOW: Long Vue Gardens and the Edgar B. Stern house. The privately owned gardens are open to the public on summer afternoons. OPPOSITE PAGE: Houmas Plantation.

PAGE 94, TOP: Jazz musicians at Commander's Palace. BOTTOM: Mile-High Ice-Cream Pie, melon with strawberries, gumbo, Red Fish Courtbouillon, and *café brûlot* —a still life photographed at the Pontchartrain Hotel. PAGE 95: Loggia of Pitot House.

Mardi Gras Day floats. TOP, LEFT: The King of Rex offers the traditional toast to his queen. OPPOSITE PAGE: King Zulu, leader of the traditional black parade, on his Mardi Gras Day float. PAGES 98 AND 99: Band following the Rex parade.

Mardi Gras maskers.

Roark Bradford's home at 719 Toulouse Street.

Restoration and Renewal: The French Quarter

While New Orleans expanded and other districts became more fashionable, the French Quarter remained abandoned and neglected until writers rediscovered it in the 1920s, moving in and restoring its buildings as homes. As it became a focal point for literary and artistic activity, the old center of the city developed the romantic cachet of the Paris Latin Quarter, with which its name has often been confused. Thus the value and charm of its historic buildings were recognized, and much of the Quarter was rescued before it could slide irrevocably into oblivion. Today a number of the fine old houses have resumed their former function as elegant private homes, others have been faithfully restored and are open to the public as museums, and many have been turned into apartments.

Roark Bradford and Lyle Saxon, both leaders of the literary life in New Orleans during its height in the 1920s and 1930s, were two of the writers who led the way to living in the disreputable, dilapidated, and disdained "Frenchtown," lending it a fashionable patina derived from the artistic work it inspired. A literary magazine called *The Double Dealer* that appeared in the Quarter between 1921 and 1926 published early work by Ernest Hemingway, William Faulkner, Edmund Wilson, and Sherwood Anderson. Both Faulkner and Anderson lived in the Quarter at that time, and Faulkner's first book was written in the Vieux Carré.

Roark Bradford's home was at 719 Toulouse Street, in a Creole cottage typical of the style of house built in the Vieux Carré after the fires of the late eighteenth century. Bradford was no more a black than George Washington Cable was a Creole, but he possessed a great talent for capturing the black spirit, style, humor, and speech patterns. Just as Cable failed in his efforts to write about anything other than Creoles, Roark Bradford's one attempt at writing a book about white people was a total flop. His fame and immortality were inadvertently transferred to Marc Connelly, whose adaptation of a Bradford novel called *Ol' Man Adam an' His Chillun* became a highly successful show called *Green Pastures.*

Saxon and Bradford, permanent residents of New Orleans whose writing was entirely regional, attracted every famous visiting writer, as well as celebrities in other fields, to their perpetual literary salons. All night, every night, the cottage on Toulouse Street, which appears so small and unprepossessing, was the scene of gatherings that included famous names of the era: Sinclair Lewis, J. B. Priestley, Louis Bromfield, Edna Ferber, Alexander Woollcott, and Gertrude Stein, among others.

Saxon, author of *Fabulous New Orleans, Old Louisiana,* and *Lafitte the Pirate,* once owned a Vieux Carré house on Madison Street, but he spent the last years of his life in the now demolished St. Charles Hotel. Saxon's protégé, Robert Tallant, produced many fine books about New Orleans in the 1940s and 1950s, but the spate of creativity that gushed forth in the 1920s and 1930s seems to have completely dried up.

Among the beautiful Vieux Carré structures now open to the public as museums is Gallier House, built by architect James Gallier, Jr., as his family home. Gallier's father, who came to New Orleans from Ireland, had established a reputation as a major architect and had designed the City Hall in Lafayette Square now known as Gallier Hall. His eyesight began to fail, and in 1849 he turned his business over to his son. By the time James Gallier, Jr., built his home in 1857 in the 1100 block of Royal Street, he had a

ABOVE AND OPPOSITE: Parlor and courtyard of Gallier House.

wife and four daughters and was a man of substantial means. He did not live long to enjoy his elegant home, for he died in 1868 at the age of forty-one, in the same year that his parents were lost in a shipwreck at sea. The Gallier family moved out in 1913, and the house was left to the creeping decay that overtook the Quarter, serving as a rooming house, with a barber shop in the carriageway. It was rescued by Mr. and Mrs. Richard Freeman, Jr., after someone showed them the empty, dilapidated building and suggested that they buy and restore it as their home. The splendid fluted Corinthian columns, elaborate plasterwork, iron lace-trimmed balcony, summer covers for fireplaces were all still there but in need of repair and restoration. In 1965 the Freemans began the work that took a year and a half, decorating the restored nineteenth-century interiors with strong, bright colors as a background for their contemporary furniture.

112

Once they began living in the house, they were so inundated with visitors anxious to see a restored Vieux Carré home that the finish on the hallway floor was worn through. After visiting Charleston's and Savannah's historic homes, Mrs. Freeman began to think that perhaps this house should be open to the public. When they had moved into the house, their children had been babies, but as they began growing up, with their school and friends uptown, living in the French Quarter caused a considerable transportation problem. So the Freemans decided to move, and the house was sold to the Ella West Freeman Foundation, to be redecorated in the style of the period in which the Galliers first lived there, and opened as a house museum.

An extensive inventory made at Gallier's death guided the furnishing and decoration of the house. Based on these records and other research, an intensive effort has been made to show exactly how people lived in nineteenth-century New Orleans, even to following the custom of changing the decoration in summer by adding slipcovers and removing rugs. Of particular interest is the huge cypress cistern in the rear of the garden, which fed the early hot-and-cold-water system devised for the Galliers' second-floor bathroom. This cistern, which was brought from a Louisiana plantation to replace the missing original, was typical of the era when New Orleanians were unaware that they were innocently breeding deadly yellow-fever-carrying mosquitoes in their own backyards.

At Gallier House excellent short films are shown on the making of ironwork and plaster cornices, and there are relevant exhibits on the top floor. At the end of the tour the visitor may sit on the balcony overlooking Royal Street while enjoying refreshments.

The home of United States Representative Lindy Boggs is one of the few French Quarter houses that have not been converted to apartments or restored as museums. Typical of dwellings constructed under the Spanish regime, the house at 623 Bourbon Street was built by Don Estaban de Quinones in 1795, the same year in which Don Almonaster y Roxas built the St. Louis Cathedral. Quinones, born in Havana in 1750, followed the Creole tradition by marrying a Frenchwoman, Marie Durieux de Dupré. After serving as secretary to the Archbishop, Quinones was appointed by the King of Spain to serve as Royal Secretary and Notary Public of the Indies. When he died in 1815, he was buried in a tomb in St. Louis Cemetery No. 1.

The Quinones house was one of the few built without business offices; therefore the first floor would have been used for storage or other utilitarian purposes. Its façade, embellished with ironwork brackets supporting the second-story gallery, is dominated by the massive arched doorway of the carriage-way, which leads to a lovely walled garden in the rear. A two-story arched loggia across the back of the house provides a tranquil vista of delightful greenery overlooking the courtyard and the *garçonnière* that encloses the rear boundary of the property. From the upper front windows of the house, the rooftops of the Vieux Carré and the busy life of Bourbon Street are visible.

Representative Boggs, who inherited the property from an aunt, has decorated the house in that period of the nineteenth century when François Seignouret was making distinctively curved dining chairs, and Prudent Mallard was turning out elaborately carved, monumental half-tester beds.

Unique in the Vieux Carré is the Hermann-Grima house at 820 St. Louis Street; it shows the American influence that followed the Louisiana Purchase and combines Georgian architecture with the Creole plan. It also clearly indicates the affluence of Samuel Hermann, the wealthy German immigrant who built it in 1831, and beautifully illustrates the life-style of a well-to-do family in New Orleans' golden age from 1830 to 1860. The house had every convenience known at the time, as well as many fine details. Exquisite fanlights and sidelights at the front door are repeated in a matching door on the second floor; interior double transoms have cast-lead decorations on their graceful woodwork. An unusual brass newel post at

BELOW: Courtyard of the Boggs house from the carriageway. RIGHT: The garconnière and fountain from the rear gallery. OPPOSITE: Nineteenth-century tester beds in the bedrooms.

OVERLEAF: Views of the Hermann-Grima house: a bedroom, the courtyard, and the Georgian façade.

Parlor ceiling medallion of Beauregard House (opposite). Built in 1867 and restored by Frances Parkinson Keyes, the house is now open to the public.

the foot of the lovely curving stairway sports a Civil War bullet hole. Unlike many other Vieux Carré dwellings, this house never had a ground-floor shop or business office. The courtyard, one of the largest in the French Quarter, has extensive outbuildings, including an extremely large three-story *garçonnière* and service wing, as well as some unclassified structures.

Samuel Hermann, an immigrant who achieved prosperity as a commission merchant after his arrival from Germany, followed the typical Creole pattern. He married a woman of French descent and christened all his children except Samuel, Jr., with French first names: Marie Virginie, Florest, Valsin, Louis Florien, and Lucien. Hermann lost his fortune in 1844, and the house was sold to a prominent Creole notary, Felix Grima. It remained in Grima's family for five generations, until it became the property of the Christian Woman's Exchange in 1924. The house was purchased by the Exchange as rental property to provide living quarters for impecunious single women and widows, and a shop for the sale of jams, preserves, and other merchandise made by women, as well as family china, silver, and other antiques.

After the house was damaged by Hurricane Betsy, architect Sam Wilson urged the Exchange to restore it. The women who work as volunteers for the Exchange began doing research and restoration in the garden and the kitchen. They became increasingly involved and eventually determined upon a serious, authentic, thoroughly researched effort. While some of their tenants remained in upstairs rooms, they began restoring the lower floors of the house, rear wing, and garden, opening the building to the public while the work was in progress.

The volunteers researched and stripped paint themselves and drafted their husbands into bricklaying and other manual labor. They succeeded in attracting not only contributions of original period furniture and paintings but also the donation of the reconstructed six-thousand-gallon cast-iron cistern on its site in the rear of the garden. Some of the original furniture remained in the house; other pieces, including family portraits, have been returned.

The garden has been stocked with fragrant plants that were popular in the period, as it would have been when the Hermanns lived there. The horse and pony stalls in the adjacent stables (added by Mr. Grima) have been restored, even though the building is used as the Exchange shop. After the kitchen had been completely finished and decorated, it was learned that its original form had been altered when an iron stove was installed to replace the cooking fireplace. So the kitchen was torn apart again in a thorough excavation to take it back to its earliest period. Discovery of the original cooking fireplace, ovens, and stew holes made possible the only authentic restoration of a Creole kitchen. A team of students from the University of New Orleans helped in the kitchen excavation and also undertook an extensive archaeological dig in the courtyard. There they unearthed foundations of an eighteenth-century building, and the largest collection of eighteenth-century ceramic pieces ever found in the city, as well as a "settling pool" adjacent to the cistern, where foods and beverages were once placed for cooling.

For their fourth annual fund-raising party in 1975, the organization chose the birthday of Marie Virginie Hermann to celebrate their acquisition of her sixteenth-birthday portrait by Jean J. Vaudechamp. All the flower arrangements and food were carefully researched and meticulously re-created as they would have been at her birthday party in 1832. A splendid array of sweetmeats, decorated cakes, pink peppermint roses, and strawberry trees was placed in the candlelit Hermann dining room. The handsome period red-and-gold draperies and upholstery in the dining room and parlor were furnished by the Colonial Dames.

In the front room across the central hall a rosewood and mahogany half-tester bed has beautifully made finials on the footboard that may be pulled up to support the end of a mosquito net that hangs behind the headboard. Next to the bed is a *prie-Dieu,* and on the night table is a *veilleuse théière,* a little ceramic

Courtyard and double parlor of Beauregard House.

stand to hold a candle under a small teapot, which thus provides both a night light and readily available hot tea. Additional furnishings and decoration continue to be added to the house in this ongoing restoration, and well-informed guides conduct tours and answer questions.

At 1113 Chartres Street is the Beauregard house built in 1826 by Joseph Le Carpentier, a French auctioneer, on land purchased from the Ursulines, whose convent is directly across the street. Spaniard Francisco Correjolles designed the building, combining Palladian architectural elements with the Louisiana raised-cottage style. The brilliant chess master Paul Morphy was born in the house in 1837, the son of Le Carpentier's daughter and Judge Alonzo Morphy.

It became known as Beauregard House when the Confederate hero rented rooms there following the Civil War. General Pierre Gustave Toutant Beauregard, a native of New Orleans, had been serving as superintendent of the military academy at West Point when Louisiana seceded from the Union in 1861. He resigned the post to become brigadier general in the Confederate Army, leading the attack on Fort Sumter that launched the war. Beauregard played a leading role at Bull Run and Shiloh, among other battles, and is as highly regarded in New Orleans as Robert E. Lee (he is commemorated by an equestrian statue at the entrance to City Park). He brought his second wife as a bride to the house in Chartres Street. After the war, during which she died, he came back to the house for a brief period as a lodger. He was a poor man in 1865,

Madame John's Legacy. OPPOSITE: A room off the front gallery. ABOVE: The Dumaine Street facade. RIGHT: The courtyard.

his career shattered along with the cause he had served. He later held several important posts in Louisiana and wrote three books on the Civil War. He died in 1893 and is buried in a tomb in Metairie Cemetery.

The house passed through many ownerships and in 1925 narrowly escaped conversion to a macaroni factory. A group of citizens formed the Beauregard Memorial Association to rescue it. Little restoration work was done until novelist Frances Parkinson Keyes bought it in 1944 and commissioned architects Koch and Wilson to restore it. She furnished it with original Beauregard pieces and memorabilia, as well as her own collections, including an amazing variety of *veilleuses théières.* Mrs. Keyes used the house as her winter residence and, while living there, wrote many books with a Louisiana background, most notably *Dinner at Antoine's.* When she died a quarter of a century later, she left Beauregard House as a museum, open to the public.

The intriguing name "Madame John's Legacy," by which the house at 632 Dumaine Street has been known for many years, promises a fascinating history, but one which, as far as fact is concerned, unfortunately remains unfulfilled. George Washington Cable used the house as a setting for one of his famous Creole stories, "'Tite Poulette," and the fictional role it played, as Madame John's Legacy, became permanently attached to the real structure. Its actual history has always been somewhat vague. There were buildings on the site as early as 1722, but the present dwelling was not erected until 1788, by Manuel DeLanzos, just after the first fire. There is little else remaining that predates that time.

The house, an unusual style of building for the Vieux Carré, is a very good example of a Creole raised cottage, with its dwelling elevated above a brick-paved first floor that was devoted to storage space. The purpose behind this prevalent regional style was to remove the living quarters from the constant threat of dampness, floods, and reptiles. The back of the house, with its gallery enclosed at either end to form small "cabinets," and its service wing with an unusual double stairway, surrounds a typical Creole courtyard.

125

Royal Street. In the center is the Merieult House.

Galleries facing the courtyard of the Merieult House.

Detail of the house shown opposite.

After serving as a home for many years, and later being rented as several apartments, Madame John's was acquired by the Louisiana State Museum, which undertook extensive restoration. Furnished with early Louisiana pieces, it is now open to the public as an example of eighteenth-century New Orleans life-style.

The Merieult house at 533 Royal Street, like Madame John's Legacy, is one of New Orleans' earliest surviving buildings, and one of the few that escaped the fire of 1794. Jean François Merieult conformed to Vieux Carré custom by building his residence above the ground-floor business offices from which he ran his worldwide shipping company.

In the 1930s General and Mrs. Kemper Williams acquired the house as part of a complex of three adjacent buildings. The wealthy and socially prominent Williamses made their elegant home in one of the houses hidden in the rear of the Merieult courtyard, where once stood the Merieult stables. The stables had been torn down and replaced by a two-story building, which was remodeled as a home in 1878 by a family who bought the Merieult house for use as a small hotel. General and Mrs. Williams retained distinguished architect Richard Koch to restore this rear building as their home, and the Merieult house as exhibition galleries for their magnificent collection of New Orleans paintings, prints, maps, books, and historical documents. The architectural details of this early structure were carefully restored to serve as a background for material on such subjects as the Battle of New Orleans, plantation life, the river, and the Cotton Centennial, each of which occupies a room of its own.

General and Mrs. Williams left the Merieult house, the Historic New Orleans Collection, and their own home as a museum. Special exhibits are housed in the street-floor galleries that were Merieult's eighteenth-century offices, and the ten upstairs rooms display the Williams collection. A splendid long ballroom used to be Merieult's counting room. The Williams home, at the rear of the beautiful interior courtyard, is maintained just as it was when General and Mrs. Williams lived there. It is filled with their fine English and French furniture, *objets d'art,* paintings and rare books, fresh flowers, and appropriate holiday decorations.

One of the few French Quarter buildings that have not been altered from their original forms is at 830 Royal Street. The house is typical of those built in the post-fire period, with shops below and residences

Handsomely restored house in Ursuline Street in the French Quarter.

above. Constructed between 1810 and 1820, with law offices on the street level, it had passed through only three ownerships when it was taken over in 1969 by James D. Didier and restored as a home for his family and as a place of business. The first owners, a French family, moved back to France. For a period it was a tinsmith's shop, and old ladies who lived on the upper floors used to lower baskets on ropes to hoist up their purchases from street venders. The building was vacant from ten to fifteen years before it was bought by Didier, a young Creole with artistic talent and impeccable taste who deals in eighteenth- and nineteenth-century Louisiana furniture and paintings. Didier considers it one of the finest buildings in New Orleans, and judges its courtyard stairway to be the most exceptional of all the curving loggia stairs in the Vieux Carré.

Although it was in the worst possible shape, Didier found all the original details of the house intact, including double ram's-horn hinges throughout the building, early carved wood wrap-around mantels, and massive pegged attic beams. Doing most of the work themselves, Didier and his partner restored the building and furnished it with the Didiers' extraordinary collection of early Louisiana antiques. The family lived here until they moved to the Pitot house (page 67).

Views of the Didier house at 830 Royal Street: the breakfast room, an attic bedroom, and the stairway in the loggia
off the courtyard.

Index